Upper-Grade Phonics

A Discovery Approach to Investigating Language Patterns

Written by Joyce A. Cockson,
Sarah McFadden Fornara,
Jan Martin, and Norm Sneller

Editor: Joel Kupperstein
Illustrator: Corbin Hillam
Cover Illustrator: Tim Huhn
Designers: Terri Lamadrid, Moonhee Pak
Cover Designer: Barbara Peterson
Art Director: Tom Cochrane
Project Director: Carolea Williams

Table of Contents

Introduction

In English, the letter *y* can make four different sounds. To a young person attempting to read or spell, complications such as this can be maddening. If *cry* is pronounced /crī/, why isn't *happy* pronounced /happī/? And why isn't *rhythm* pronounced /rīthm/? Fortunately for these young readers, the pronunciation of *y* follows a pattern. Learning this pattern provides a key to reading and spelling the dozens of English words spelled with *y*. Can we call this pattern a rule? No. Too many words, like *rhyme* and *justify*, do not conform. Still, the pattern holds in a vast majority of cases.

Research shows the human brain is a much more effective pattern recognizer than it is a rule memorizer. Given exposure to and practice with a pattern, the brain can quickly apply the pattern to unfamiliar but similar circumstances. Because of the brain's knack for patterns, we are able to cope with new situations, even outside the scope of reading. For example, the brain establishes patterns as it encounters machines such as cars and microwave ovens, and, as a result, people have an idea how to operate other cars and microwave ovens, even if these machines are slightly different than their own. Establishing patterns of language and familiarizing students with them is the exact purpose of this book. Introducing students to the language patterns featured in this book will increase their facility with all aspects of literacy, including reading, writing, vocabulary expansion, and comprehension.

A Discovery Approach

Frequently, explicit, direct phonics instruction ends with the presentation of a phonics concept. Students may then require many separate follow-up experiences to make the concept meaningful and to apply it to real reading. Unfortunately, the limitations of younger students' cognitive abilities and attention spans often necessitate this approach to incite learning. Upper-grade teachers, on the other hand, have the luxury of their students' advanced maturity and cognitive skills and can be more creative in their instructional approach, even when the curriculum is basic or remedial. The discovery approach is one such teaching methodology upper-grade students benefit from and enjoy when learning remedial, basic, or advanced phonics and language patterns. The discovery approach is one of the many key features of this book.

A discovery approach, whether it is applied to science experiments, math concepts, or language patterns, presents students with

raw materials or data and challenges them to discover unifying principles. In the case of this book, students examine words that follow a pattern and draw conclusions about the nature of the pattern. Advantages of this approach include the following:

- Students' active involvement increases their motivation to participate.
- Open-ended investigations invite students to use their strengths as learners and accommodate all learning styles.
- A variety of activity formats keeps student interest high over long periods of time.
- Most importantly, the act of discovering makes the language pattern meaningful and memorable to students.

In many ways, discovering language patterns is similar to solving mysteries. Students must gather informative clues and evidence; avoid distracting, extraneous information; and draw provable conclusions. This book carries through it a mystery theme to highlight the investigative

aspects of learning about language patterns and pique students' interest in the investigations. Bring this highly motivating mystery theme to your classroom as you work with language patterns, and watch your students "devour" the materials provided in these pages.

Who Needs *Upper-Grade Phonics?*

Simply put, all students can benefit from *Upper-Grade Phonics.* Language patterns featured in this book address the needs of students who require remediation of basic concepts to on-grade-level readers to students ready to learn more advanced concepts. Even if students are somewhat familiar with a phonics concept, this book's discovery approach enables them to permanently and meaningfully embed the concept in their brains. To work with the patterns in this book, students should "bring to the table" the following knowledge and abilities:

- letter recognition
- sound/letter matching
- concepts of print such as one-to-one correspondence, reading left to right, and return sweep from line to line
- pronunciation of consonant blends and digraphs
- pronunciation of vowel digraphs and diphthongs
- familiarity with high-frequency words
- basic familiarity with sentence and story structure
- awareness of parts of speech

Once familiar with these concepts, students are ready for the language patterns and activities in this book. They are ready to become "Language Detectives."

Using This Book

The body of this book is divided into four main sections: Language Mysteries, Mini-Lessons, Solution Stretchers, and Teaching Helpers.

Language Mysteries

The Language Mysteries are the language patterns—the "raw data"—that fuel this book's discovery approach. They present the Mystery to be solved phrased as a question. The book features 47 patterns divided into three categories based on the domain of literacy they address: Decoding Mysteries (reading), Encoding Mysteries (spelling), and Word-Solving Mysteries (comprehension and vocabulary).

Decoding Mysteries include patterns that students can apply when reading print. For example, the pattern that tells whether the suffix *-ed* is pronounced /ĕd/, /d/, or /t/ is Decoding Mystery #7. The term *decoding* is often used in reference to sounding out words.

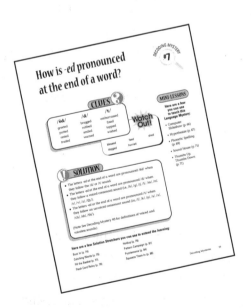

Encoding Mysteries include patterns that students can apply when spelling words they know how to pronounce. For example, the pattern that tells whether the /k/ sound is spelled *c, k,* or *ck* at the end of a word is Encoding Mystery #3. The term *encoding* is often used in reference to transferring words from oral language to written language.

Word-Solving Mysteries include patterns that students can apply when deriving the meaning or usage of unfamiliar words. For example, the pattern that tells which prefixes mean "not" or "the opposite of" is Word-Solving Mystery #4. Word-Solving Mysteries are intended to help students expand their vocabulary and increase their comprehension skills.

The next page explains the structure of a Language Mystery.

Language Mysteries
The Language Mystery question presents the language pattern to be investigated or discovered.

Clues/Watch Out!
The Clues section contains words that follow the language pattern. The Watch Out! section lists words that break the pattern or may cause confusion. Watch Out! words may differ from Clues words in their spelling, their pronunciation, or even their usage. Words in these lists are not complete lists of all English words that follow and break the pattern. Instead, they are a sampling of words that establish evidence of the pattern. Presenting Clues words must be part of teaching every language pattern, but Watch Out! words may or may not be presented, depending on the Mini-Lessons and Solution Stretchers used.

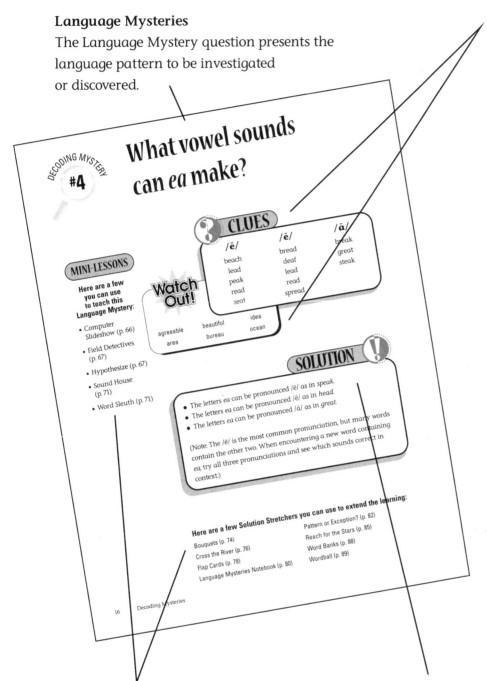

DECODING MYSTERY #4

What vowel sounds can ea make?

CLUES

/ē/
beach
lead
peak
read
seat

/ĕ/
bread
deaf
lead
read
spread

/ā/
break
great
steak

Watch Out!

agreeable   beautiful   idea   area   bureau   ocean

MINI-LESSONS

Here are a few you can use to teach this Language Mystery:

- Computer Slideshow (p. 66)
- Field Detectives (p. 67)
- Hypothesize (p. 67)
- Sound House (p. 71)
- Word Sleuth (p. 71)

SOLUTION

- The letters *ea* can be pronounced /ē/ as in *speak*.
- The letters *ea* can be pronounced /ĕ/ as in *head*.
- The letters *ea* can be pronounced /ā/ as in *great*.

(Note: The /ē/ is the most common pronunciation, but many words contain the other two. When encountering a new word containing *ea*, try all three pronunciations and see which sounds correct in context.)

Here are a few Solution Stretchers you can use to extend the learning:

Bouquets (p. 74)
Cross the River (p. 76)
Flap Cards (p. 78)
Language Mysteries Notebook (p. 80)

Pattern or Exception? (p. 82)
Reach for the Stars (p. 85)
Word Banks (p. 88)
Wordball (p. 89)

16   Decoding Mysteries

Mini-Lessons and Solution Stretchers
Each Language Mystery page lists a few Mini-Lessons and Solution Stretchers that coordinate with the Mystery. See the Sample Lesson on page 9 for a detailed example of how all these pieces fit together.

Solution
The Solution section explains the answer to the Language Mystery. Solutions cover conditions under which words are spelled, pronounced, or used according to the pattern. Solutions may be followed by notes that provide further insight into the nature of the language pattern.

Mini-Lessons and Solution Stretchers

Mini-Lessons and Solution Stretchers are easily adaptable to many language patterns. Each of the three Language Mysteries sections begins with charts detailing exactly which Mini-Lessons and Solution Stretchers coordinate with the patterns in that section. In addition, each Mystery page specifically lists several Mini-Lessons and Solution Stretchers that work particularly well with that language pattern. All Mini-Lessons and Solution Stretchers involve generating or presenting Clues words, and some also incorporate Watch Out! words. Use the Mini-Lessons to introduce a language pattern and the Solution Stretchers to provide practice and review.

Mini-Lessons

This section contains 15 ideas for presenting Language Mysteries. These ideas are adaptable to most Language Mysteries and afford you a great deal of flexibility. If your students particularly enjoy one Mini-Lesson format, use it to present several Language Mysteries. If your students struggle with a Mystery presented in one format, reteach the Mystery in a different format until they understand the pattern. These activities are intended to take 10–20 minutes.

Solution Stretchers

This section contains 32 independent, small-group, whole-group, and learning-center extension activities that provide further practice with language patterns you introduced through Mini-Lessons. Like the Mini-Lessons, these activities are adaptable to many different Language Mysteries. Unlike the Mini-Lessons, these activities fill larger amounts of time and reinforce, rather than introduce, the application of language patterns.

Teaching Helpers

This section features helpful tools that can be used before and during phonics instruction. The first two sections are pre-assessments to gauge students' phonics knowledge and basic literacy skills. The remaining three sections are word lists you may wish to reproduce for students, convert to wall charts, and/or keep for your own reference. Having these lists of commonly confused words, commonly misspelled words, and homophones gives you and your students a handy resource for solving problems posed by the English language that are not addressed by an identifiable pattern.

Sample Lesson

This section provides an example of how one Language Mystery might be presented to a class using the Mini-Lessons and Solution Stretchers in this resource.

1. **Select a Language Mystery**
   The teacher selects Decoding Mystery #2 (the sounds of *y*, page 14) to present to the class.

2. **Select and Prepare a Mini-Lesson**
   Based on the recommendation on the Mystery page, the teacher decides to introduce the pattern using the Card Sort Mini-Lesson activity (page 65). The teacher prepares five sets of twelve index cards. Each set of cards contains the same three examples of words featuring each of the four sounds *y* can make: /ē/, /ĭ/, /ī/, and the consonant *y* sound (/y/).

3. **Present the Mini-Lesson**
   The teacher divides the class into five groups and gives each group a set of twelve cards. The teacher invites the groups to take a few minutes to sort the cards into any categories they see fit. When some groups appear to struggle, the teacher recommends that they focus on the letter *y* in each word. The groups then share their sorting strategies, and the teacher guides them toward recognizing the four sounds *y* can make and the patterns related to those sounds.

4. **Select a Solution Stretcher**
   Some time has passed, and the teacher decides students need additional practice with the "sounds of *y*" pattern. After scanning the chart on page 12, the teacher chooses to reinforce the pattern using the Holdup Solution Stretcher activity (page 79).

5. **Implement the Solution Stretcher**
   The teacher gives students four index cards each and asks them to write one of the following notations on each of the cards: *y* = /ē/, *y* = /ĭ/, *y* = /ī/, and *y* = /y/. The teacher displays several words containing *y*, each time challenging students to hold up the card that indicates the sound *y* makes in that word. The teacher continues the activity until students clearly demonstrate understanding of the pattern.

Pronunciation Symbols

Throughout this book, the phonetic pronunciation of letters and words is written enclosed in slashes. The symbols and sounds incorporated in these phonetic spellings are

/ă/ as in bat	/oi/ as in join
/ā/ as in rain	/ōl/ as in cold
/är/ as in farm	/ôl/ as in halt
/aů/ as in now	/ōr/ as in port
/ch/ as in chip	/sh/ as in shall
/ĕ/ as in red	/<u>th</u>/ as in that
/ē/ as in weep	/th/ as in thin
/ĭ/ as in tin	/ŭ/ as in run
/ī/ as in hide	/ü/ as in tooth
/kw/ as in quack	/ů/ as in wood
/ŏ/ as in not	/ůl/ as in pull
/ō/ as in boat	/ŭr/ as in curse
/ô/ as in broth	

Consonant sounds are indicated phonetically by the consonant that most frequently makes that sound. For example, /f/ is used for words spelled with f or ph, and /s/ is used for words spelled with s or c.

(Note: English dialects may affect the pronunciation of words. Be sure to consider students' dialects when teaching phonics patterns and phonetic spelling.)

Decoding Mysteries (Reading)

Decoding Mysteries include patterns that students can apply when reading print. For example, the pattern that tells whether the suffix -ed is pronounced /ĕd/, /d/, or /t/ appears in this section (Decoding Mystery #7). The term *decoding* is often used in reference to sounding out words.

This table shows which **Mini-Lessons** can be used to introduce each Decoding Mystery.

Decoding Mystery #	Around the Circle (p. 65)	Card Sort (p. 65)	Computer Slideshow (p. 66)	Does It Belong? (p. 66)	Field Detectives (p. 67)	Hypothesize (p. 67)	In My Bag (p. 68)	Name That Mystery (p. 68)	Open Forum (p. 69)	Phonetic Spelling (p. 69)	Riddles (p. 70)	Secret Boxes (p. 70)	Sound House (p. 71)	Thumbs Up, Thumbs Down (p. 71)	Word Sleuth (p. 71)
1	X	X	X	X	X	X	X	X	X	X	X	X	X	X	
2	X	X	X	X	X	X	X	X	X	X	X	X	X	X	X
3	X	X	X	X	X	X	X	X	X	X		X	X	X	X
4	X	X	X	X	X	X	X	X	X	X		X	X	X	X
5	X	X	X	X	X	X	X	X	X	X		X	X	X	X
6	X	X	X	X	X	X	X	X	X	X		X	X	X	X
7	X	X	X	X	X	X	X	X	X	X		X	X	X	
8	X	X	X	X	X	X	X	X	X	X		X	X	X	X
9	X	X	X	X	X	X	X	X	X	X		X	X	X	X
10		X	X	X			X	X	X	X	X	X	X	X	X
11	X		X		X		X	X	X	X		X	X	X	X
12	X	X	X	X	X		X	X	X	X		X	X	X	X
13	X	X	X	X	X	X	X	X	X	X		X	X	X	X
14	X	X	X	X	X		X	X		X	X	X	X	X	X
15	X	X	X	X	X		X	X		X	X	X	X	X	X
16		X	X	X	X	X	X					X	X	X	
17		X	X		X	X						X	X		
18		X	X		X	X						X	X		
19		X	X		X							X	X		

This table shows which **Solution Stretchers** can be used with each Decoding Mystery.

Decoding Mystery #	Banners (p.73)	Board Games (p.73)	Bouquets (p.74)	Buzz In (p.74)	Catching Words (p.75)	Cross the River (p.76)	Discussion Session (p.76)	Dungeon Keeper (p.77)	Fill the Basket (p.77)	Flap Cards (p.78)	Flash Card Relay (p.78)	Highlighter Hunt (p.79)	Holdup (p.79)	Kinesthetic Spelling (p.80)	Lang. Mysteries Notebook (p.80)	Mystery Montage (p.81)	Pattern Campaign (p.81)	Pattern Links (p.82)	Pattern or Exception? (p.82)	Pizza Slices (p.83)	Puzzlemania (p.84)	Raining Rules (p.84)	Reach for the Stars (p.85)	Reference Books (p.85)	Single Elimination (p.86)	Squeeze Them In (p.86)	Swat It! (p.87)	Tic-Tac-Toe (p.87)	The Way Out (p.88)	Word Banks (p.88)	Word Roots (p.89)	Wordball (p.89)
1	x	x	x	x	x	x	x	x	x	x	x	x	x	x	x	x	x	x	x		x	x	x	x	x	x	x	x	x	x	x	x
2	x	x	x	x	x	x	x	x	x	x	x	x	x	x	x	x	x	x	x		x	x	x	x	x	x	x	x	x	x	x	x
3	x	x	x	x	x	x	x	x			x	x	x		x		x	x	x		x	x	x	x	x	x	x	x	x	x	x	x
4	x	x	x	x		x	x	x	x	x	x	x	x	x	x	x	x	x	x		x	x	x	x	x	x	x	x	x	x	x	x
5	x	x	x	x		x	x	x	x	x	x	x	x	x	x	x	x	x	x		x	x	x	x	x	x	x	x	x	x	x	x
6	x	x	x	x		x	x	x	x	x	x	x	x	x	x	x	x	x	x		x	x	x	x	x	x	x	x	x	x	x	x
7	x	x	x	x	x	x	x	x			x	x	x		x	x	x	x	x	x	x	x	x	x	x	x	x	x	x	x	x	x
8	x	x	x	x		x	x	x	x	x	x	x	x	x	x	x	x			x	x	x	x	x	x	x	x	x	x	x		x
9	x	x	x	x		x	x	x	x	x	x	x	x	x	x	x	x			x	x	x	x	x	x	x	x	x	x	x	x	x
10	x	x			x	x	x	x	x	x	x	x			x	x	x	x	x		x	x	x	x	x	x		x	x	x	x	x
11	x	x			x	x	x	x	x	x	x	x			x	x	x	x	x		x	x	x	x	x	x		x	x	x	x	x
12	x	x	x		x	x	x	x	x	x	x	x			x	x	x	x	x	x	x	x	x	x	x	x		x	x	x	x	x
13	x	x	x	x		x	x	x	x	x	x	x	x	x	x	x	x	x	x		x	x	x	x	x	x	x	x	x	x	x	x
14	x	x	x	x		x	x	x	x	x	x	x	x	x	x	x	x			x		x		x	x	x	x	x	x	x		x
15	x	x	x	x		x	x	x	x	x	x	x	x	x	x	x	x	x		x		x	x	x	x	x		x	x	x		x
16		x	x		x		x	x	x				x		x		x	x			x				x	x	x	x	x			x
17		x	x		x	x	x	x			x		x	x		x	x			x		x	x	x	x			x		x		
18		x	x		x	x	x	x			x		x	x		x	x			x		x	x	x	x			x		x		
19		x	x		x	x	x	x	x		x	x		x		x	x			x		x	x	x	x			x		x		

When does *c* make the /s/ sound and when does it make the /k/ sound? When does *g* make the /j/ sound and when does it make the /g/ sound?

DECODING MYSTERY #1

CLUES

c = /s/	c = /k/	g = /j/	g = /g/
acid	acre	age	dog
cent	call	badge	gaze
cider	cane	genius	glad
circus	cap	gentle	goat
citrus	clean	giant	gone
dance	coat	ginger	greet
receive	cut	gym	gutter
source	record	spongy	regal

Watch Out!

cello	gear	girl
foggy	gift	tangy

MINI-LESSONS

Here are a few you can use to teach this Language Mystery:

- Card Sort (p. 65)
- Does It Belong? (p. 66)
- Name That Mystery (p. 68)
- Secret Boxes (p. 70)
- Thumbs Up, Thumbs Down (p. 71)

SOLUTION

- *C* is pronounced /k/ and *g* is pronounced /g/ when they precede *a, o, u,* or any consonant. These are known as the "hard *c* and *g* sounds."
- *C* is pronounced /s/ and *g* is pronounced /j/ when they precede the letter *i, e,* or *y*. These are known as the "soft *c* and *g* sounds."

Here are a few Solution Stretchers you can use to extend the learning:

How many sounds can the letter y make? When does it make each sound?

CLUES

/y/	/ĭ/	/ī/	/ē/
yak	cymbal	cry	any
yawn	cyst	fly	dirty
yell	hymn	sky	every
yes	symbol	try	happy
you	synonym	why	pony

MINI-LESSONS

Here are a few you can use to teach this Language Mystery:

- Card Sort (p. 65)
- Open Forum (p. 69)
- Riddles (p. 70)
- Sound House (p. 71)
- Word Sleuth (p. 71)

Watch Out!

justify	myself	rhyme	toy
myrrh	mystify	stay	tray

SOLUTION

- *Y* at the beginning of a word is a consonant. It makes the /y/ sound.
- *Y* in the middle of a word makes the /ĭ/ sound.
- *Y* at the end of a one-syllable word makes the /ī/ sound.
- *Y* at the end of a polysyllabic word makes the /ē/ sound.

Here are a few Solution Stretchers you can use to extend the learning:

Banners (p. 73)

Buzz In (p. 74)

Dungeon Keeper (p. 77)

Holdup (p. 79)

Pizza Slices (p. 83)

Reference Books (p. 85)

Swat It! (p. 87)

Word Roots (p. 89)

When does *s* at the end of a word make the /z/ sound and when does it make the /s/ sound?

CLUES

/s/	/s/	/z/
bus	bats	bags
gas	cups	cards
less	lights	keys
yes	sticks	wins

Watch Out!

as	has	is	use	was

MINI-LESSONS

Here are a few you can use to teach this Language Mystery:

- Around the Circle (p. 65)
- Computer Slideshow (p. 66)
- Hypothesize (p. 67)
- In My Bag (p. 68)
- Open Forum (p. 69)

SOLUTION

- In words ending in *s*, where *s* is not a suffix, the *s* is pronounced /s/.
- In words with an *s* suffix (e.g., plural nouns and singular verbs), *s* is pronounced /s/ when it follows an unvoiced consonant sound (i.e., /f/, /k/, /p/, /s/, /ch/, /sh/, /th/).
- In words with an *s* suffix (e.g., plural nouns and singular verbs), *s* is pronounced /z/ when it follows a voiced consonant sound (i.e., /b/, /g/, /j/, /l/, /m/, /n/, /r/, /v/, /z/, /th/) or a vowel sound.

(Note: Voiced sounds require vibration of the vocal cords. Voiceless sounds do not. For example, the sounds /s/ and /z/ are made with the mouth in the same position. For the /z/ sound, the vocal cords vibrate—they do not vibrate for the /s/ sound. Therefore, /z/ is voiced and /s/ is voiceless.)

Here are a few Solution Stretchers you can use to extend the learning:

Buzz In (p. 74)

Catching Words (p. 75)

Fill the Basket (p. 77)

Highlighter Hunt (p. 79)

Mystery Montage (p. 81)

Pizza Slices (p. 83)

Single Elimination (p. 86)

The Way Out (p. 88)

What vowel sounds can *ea* make?

MINI-LESSONS

Here are a few you can use to teach this Language Mystery:

- Computer Slideshow (p. 66)
- Field Detectives (p. 67)
- Hypothesize (p. 67)
- Sound House (p. 71)
- Word Sleuth (p. 71)

CLUES

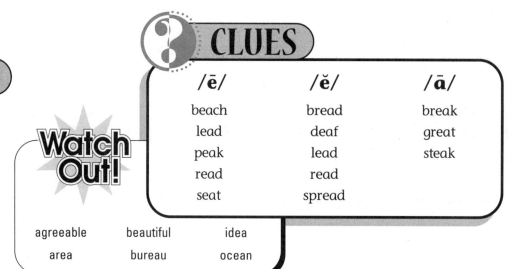

/ē/	/ĕ/	/ā/
beach	bread	break
lead	deaf	great
peak	lead	steak
read	read	
seat	spread	

Watch Out!

agreeable   beautiful   idea

area   bureau   ocean

SOLUTION

- The letters *ea* can be pronounced /ē/ as in *speak*.
- The letters *ea* can be pronounced /ĕ/ as in *head*.
- The letters *ea* can be pronounced /ā/ as in *great*.

(Note: The /ē/ is the most common pronunciation, but many words contain the other two. When encountering a new word containing *ea*, try all three pronunciations and see which sounds correct in context.)

Here are a few Solution Stretchers you can use to extend the learning:

What sounds can *oo* make?

CLUES ?

/ ů/		/ü/	
book	look	bloom	school
cook	shook	droop	shampoo
foot	stood	groom	stool
hood	wool	moon	tooth

Watch Out!

blood	floor
brooch	hooray

MINI-LESSONS

Here are a few you can use to teach this Language Mystery:

- Around the Circle (p. 65)
- Card Sort (p. 65)
- Name That Mystery (p. 68)
- Riddles (p. 70)
- Word Sleuth (p. 71)

SOLUTION

- The letters *oo* can be pronounced /ů/ as in *wood*.
- The letters *oo* can be pronounced /ü/ as in *room*.

(Note: When encountering a new word containing *oo*, try both pronunciations and see which sounds correct in context.)

Here are a few Solution Stretchers you can use to extend the learning:

Banners (p. 73)

Discussion Session (p. 76)

Highlighter Hunt (p. 79)

Mystery Montage (p. 81)

Raining Rules (p. 84)

Single Elimination (p. 86)

Tic-Tac-Toe (p. 87)

The Way Out (p. 88)

What sounds can ough make?

MINI-LESSONS

Here are a few you can use to teach this Language Mystery:

- Does It Belong? (p. 66)
- Field Detectives (p. 67)
- In My Bag (p. 68)
- Open Forum (p. 69)
- Secret Boxes (p. 70)

CLUES

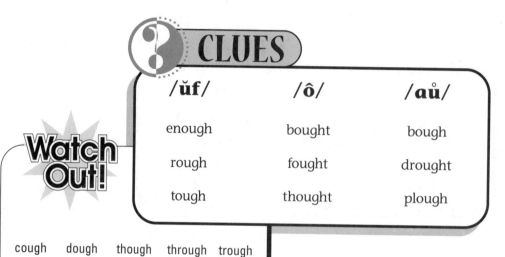

Watch Out!

/ŭf/	/ô/	/aů/
enough	bought	bough
rough	fought	drought
tough	thought	plough

cough   dough   though   through   trough

SOLUTION

- *Ough* may make the /ŭf/ sound.
- *Ough* may make the /ô/ sound.
- *Ough* may make the /aů/ sound.

(Note: The three sounds for *ough* listed above appear in the most words, but a few words contain *ough* pronounced /ôf/, /ō/, or /ü/. These pronunciations appear in few words, but some of those words, such as *cough*, *though*, and *through*, are quite common.)

Here are a few Solution Stretchers you can use to extend the learning:

Board Games (p. 73)

Bouquets (p. 74)

Flap Cards (p. 78)

Holdup (p. 79)

Pattern Links (p. 82)

Pattern or Exception? (p. 82)

Swat It! (p. 87)

Word Roots (p. 89)

How is -ed pronounced at the end of a word?

CLUES

/ĕd/	/d/	/t/
greeted	bragged	embarrassed
patted	robbed	fixed
rested	smiled	tapped
traded	warned	wished

Watch Out!

blessed	feed	shed
dogged	hurried	

MINI-LESSONS

Here are a few you can use to teach this Language Mystery:

- Computer Slideshow (p. 66)
- Hypothesize (p. 67)
- Phonetic Spelling (p. 69)
- Sound House (p. 71)
- Thumbs Up, Thumbs Down (p. 71)

SOLUTION

- The letters -ed at the end of a word are pronounced /ĕd/ when they follow the /d/ or /t/ sound.
- The letters -ed at the end of a word are pronounced /d/ when they follow a voiced consonant sound (i.e., /b/, /g/, /j/, /l/, /m/, /n/, /r/, /v/, /z/, /th/).
- The letters -ed at the end of a word are pronounced /t/ when they follow an unvoiced consonant sound (i.e., /f/, /k/, /p/, /s/, /x/, /ch/, /sh/, /th/).

(Note: See Decoding Mystery #3 for definitions of voiced and voiceless sounds.)

Here are a few Solution Stretchers you can use to extend the learning:

Buzz In (p. 74)

Catching Words (p. 75)

Fill the Basket (p. 77)

Flash Card Relay (p. 78)

Holdup (p. 79)

Pattern Campaign (p. 81)

Puzzlemania (p. 84)

Squeeze Them In (p. 86)

#8

What letters make the /f/ sound?

CLUES

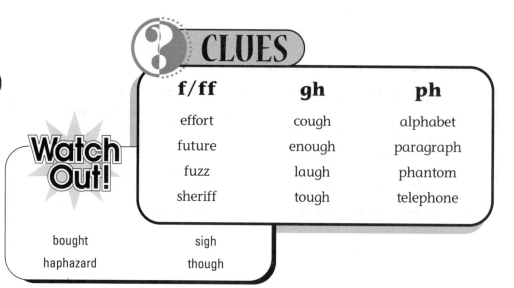

Watch Out!

f/ff	gh	ph
effort	cough	alphabet
future	enough	paragraph
fuzz	laugh	phantom
sheriff	tough	telephone

bought	sigh
haphazard	though

MINI-LESSONS

Here are a few you can use to teach this Language Mystery:

- Around the Circle (p. 65)
- Card Sort (p. 65)
- Hypothesize (p. 67)
- Open Forum (p. 69)
- Riddles (p. 70)

SOLUTION

- The letter *f,* alone or doubled, is the most common spelling of the /f/ sound.
- When following the vowel combination *au* or *ou,* the letters *gh* often make the /f/ sound, but only if they are at the end of a word. For example, *gh* in *bought* does not make the /f/ sound, but *gh* in *laugh* does.
- The letter combination *ph* is nearly always pronounced /f/.

Here are a few Solution Stretchers you can use to extend the learning:

DECODING MYSTERY #9

What letters commonly make the /ô/ sound?

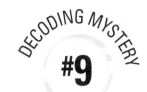

CLUES

au	*aw*	*augh*	*o*	*ough*
author	awful	daughter	frost	bought
cause	lawn	naughty	moth	fought
saucer	straw	taught	soft	ought

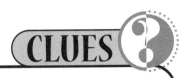

Watch Out!

aunt	cough	draught	plough
away	dough	laugh	rough

MINI-LESSONS

Here are a few you can use to teach this Language Mystery:

- Does It Belong? (p. 66)
- Field Detectives (p. 67)
- Name That Mystery (p. 68)
- Thumbs Up, Thumbs Down (p. 71)
- Word Sleuth (p. 71)

SOLUTION

- Five different letter combinations commonly make the /ô/ sound. These combinations are *au, aw, augh, o,* and *ough*. The *au* and *aw* combinations are the most regular examples. They will almost always be pronounced /ô/.

(Note: In some dialects the /ô/ sound i
sound. For example, *bought* and *pot* r

Here are a few Solution Stretchers yo

Bouquets (p. 74)

Discussion Session (p. 76)

Highlighter Hunt (p. 79)

Mystery Montage (p. 81)

-all words up-
whats in common?
-put in an order
-fill out chart

How can an *e* at the end of a word affect the word's pronunciation?

CLUES

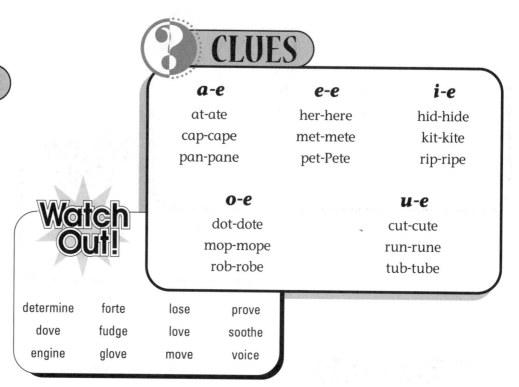

a-e	e-e	i-e
at-ate	her-here	hid-hide
cap-cape	met-mete	kit-kite
pan-pane	pet-Pete	rip-ripe

o-e	u-e
dot-dote	cut-cute
mop-mope	run-rune
rob-robe	tub-tube

Watch Out!

determine	forte	lose	prove
dove	fudge	love	soothe
engine	glove	move	voice

MINI-LESSONS

Here are a few you can use to teach this Language Mystery:

- Computer Slideshow (p. 66)
- In My Bag (p. 68)
- Phonetic Spelling (p. 69)
- Sound House (p. 71)
- Thumbs Up, Thumbs Down (p. 71)

SOLUTION

- When appearing at the end of a word and preceded by a vowel and a consonant (the V-C or C-V-C pattern), *e* is silent, but the vowel preceding it is usually long.

Here are a few Solution Stretchers you can use to extend the learning:

How are vowels at the end of short words pronounced?

DECODING MYSTERY #11

CLUES

e	i	o	u
be	pi	go	flu
he		ho	
me		lo	
she		no	
we		so	
ye			

Watch Out!

do	hello	pa	the
ha	ma	ski	to

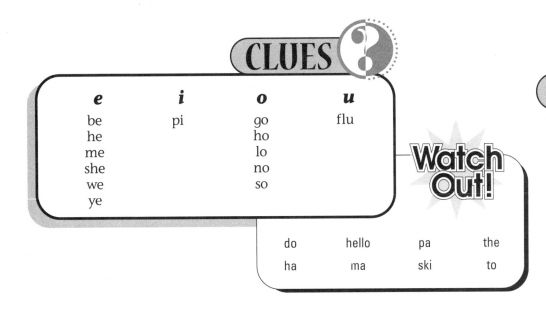

MINI-LESSONS

Here are a few you can use to teach this Language Mystery:

- Around the Circle (p. 65)
- Field Detectives (p. 67)
- Name That Mystery (p. 68)
- Open Forum (p. 69)
- Word Sleuth (p. 71)

SOLUTION

- A vowel at the end of a one-syllable word is usually pronounced as a long vowel.

(Note: This pattern holds only if the vowel at the end of the word is the only vowel in the word. Vowel combinations in words such as *sea* and silent *e* words such as *hope* do not fit this pattern.)

Here are a few Solution Stretchers you can use to extend the learning:

Banners (p. 73)

Cross the River (p. 76)

Fill the Basket (p. 77)

Language Mysteries Notebook (p. 80)

Reach for the Stars (p. 85)

Squeeze Them In (p. 86)

Word Banks (p. 88)

Wordball (p. 89)

In words where *i* and *o* are the only vowels, when are they pronounced as long vowels?

MINI-LESSONS

Here are a few you can use to teach this Language Mystery:

- Card Sort (p. 65)

- Does It Belong? (p. 66)

- Open Forum (p. 69)

- Phonetic Spelling (p. 69)

- Thumbs Up, Thumbs Down (p. 71)

CLUES

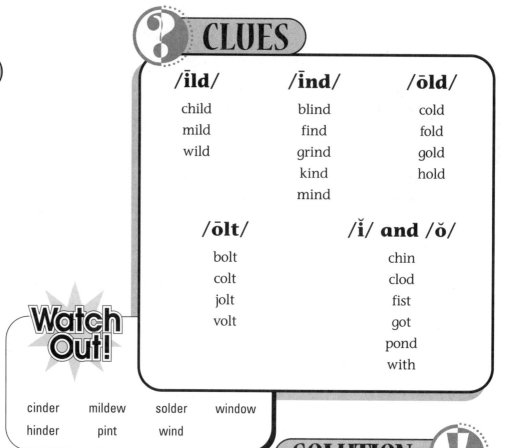

/īld/	/īnd/	/ōld/
child	blind	cold
mild	find	fold
wild	grind	gold
	kind	hold
	mind	

/ōlt/	/ĭ/ and /ŏ/
bolt	chin
colt	clod
jolt	fist
volt	got
	pond
	with

Watch Out!

cinder	mildew	solder	window
hinder	pint	wind	

SOLUTION

- *I* is usually pronounced /ī/ when it precedes *ld* or *nd*.
- *O* is usually pronounced /ō/ when it precedes *ld* or *lt*.

(Note: Words such as *now* and *slow* are not relevant to this pattern because the *ow* combination is considered a vowel digraph.)

Here are a few Solution Stretchers you can use to extend the learning:

Bouquets (p. 74)

Discussion Session (p. 76)

Dungeon Keeper (p. 77)

Kinesthetic Spelling (p. 80)

Pattern or Exception? (p. 82)

Pizza Slices (p. 83)

Reach for the Stars (p. 85)

Tic-Tac-Toe (p. 87)

What sounds do vowels make when they precede the *-ing*, *-ed*, and *-er* endings?

CLUES

single consonant	multiple consonants
diner	dinner
filing	filling
hoping	hopping
liked	licked
liking	planned
planed	pushed
shaper	shopper
super	supper
taping	tapping

Watch Out!

ceiling	coming	gnawed	power
combated	dialed	lived	skier

MINI-LESSONS

Here are a few you can use to teach this Language Mystery:

- Computer Slideshow (p. 66)
- Hypothesize (p. 67)
- In My Bag (p. 68)
- Name That Mystery (p. 68)
- Sound House (p. 71)

SOLUTION

- If one consonant separates the suffix and the vowel, the vowel before the consonant is long.
- If two or more consonants separate the suffix and the vowel, the vowel before the consonant is short.

(Note: This pattern applies only to root words whose vowel sound is made by one letter or one letter and silent *e*.)

Here are a few Solution Stretchers you can use to extend the learning:

Buzz In (p. 74)

Highlighter Hunt (p. 79)

Mystery Montage (p. 81)

Raining Rules (p. 84)

Single Elimination (p. 86)

Swat It! (p. 87)

The Way Out (p. 88)

Word Roots (p. 89)

DECODING MYSTERY #14

What consonants can be silent at the beginning of a word? When are they silent?

MINI-LESSONS

Here are a few
you can use
to teach this
Language Mystery:

- Around the Circle (p. 65)

- Field Detectives (p. 67)

- Phonetic Spelling (p. 69)

- Riddles (p. 70)

- Word Sleuth (p. 71)

? CLUES

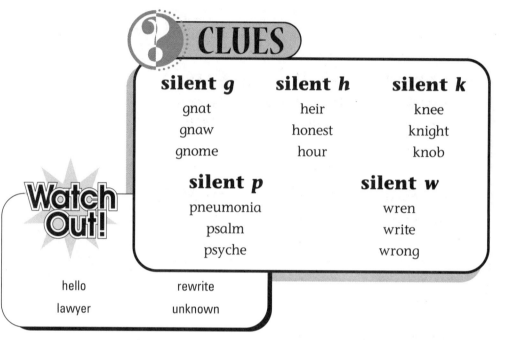

silent *g*	silent *h*	silent *k*
gnat	heir	knee
gnaw	honest	knight
gnome	hour	knob

silent *p*	silent *w*
pneumonia	wren
psalm	write
psyche	wrong

Watch Out!

hello	rewrite
lawyer	unknown

SOLUTION

- *G* is silent when it precedes *n* at the beginning of a word.
- *H* is often silent at the beginning of a word.
- *K* is silent when it precedes *n* at the beginning of a word.
- *P* is silent when it precedes *n* or *s* at the beginning of a word.
- *W* is silent when it precedes *r* at the beginning of a word.

Here are a few Solution Stretchers you can use to extend the learning:

Board Games (p. 73)

Flap Cards (p. 78)

Holdup (p. 79)

Language Mysteries Notebook (p. 80)

Pattern Campaign (p. 81)

Pattern Links (p. 82)

Reference Books (p. 85)

Word Banks (p. 88)

What consonants can be silent in the middle or at the end of a word?

CLUES

silent *b*	silent *h*	silent *n*
debt	rhinoceros	column
doubt	rhombus	hymn
limb	rhyme	solemn
plumber	rhythm	

silent *g*	silent *l*	silent *t*
campaign	calf	bustle
design	half	castle
foreign	salmon	hustle
sign		whistle

Watch Out!

chalk	khaki	palm
colonel	lumber	signature
gymnasium	often	yolk

SOLUTION

- *B* is usually silent when it follows *m* or when it precedes *t*.
- *G* is silent when it precedes *n* at the end of a word.
- *H* is often silent following *r*.
- *L* is silent when it falls between *a* and *f* at the end of a word. Depending on the dialect, *l* may be silent in the letter combinations *lk* and *lm*.
- *N* is silent when it follows *m* at the end of a word.
- *T* is silent when it falls between *s* and *le* at the end of a word.

(Note: *G* and *h* may be silent at the beginning, in the middle, or at the end of words. Some dialects consider the *h* silent when it follows *w* in words such as *whale* and *what*.)

MINI-LESSONS

Here are a few you can use to teach this Language Mystery:

- Card Sort (p. 65)
- Does It Belong? (p. 66)
- In My Bag (p. 68)
- Secret Boxes (p. 70)
- Thumbs Up, Thumbs Down (p. 71)

Here are a few Solution Stretchers you can use to extend the learning:

Buzz In (p. 74)

Cross the River (p. 76)

Discussion Session (p. 76)

Fill the Basket (p. 77)

Flash Card Relay (p. 78)

Highlighter Hunt (p. 79)

Kinesthetic Spelling (p. 80)

Squeeze Them In (p. 86)

#16

What is a syllable and how can you tell how many a word has?

MINI-LESSONS

Here are a few you can use to teach this Language Mystery:

- Card Sort (p. 65)
- Computer Slideshow (p. 66)
- Hypothesize (p. 67)
- Sound House (p. 71)
- Thumbs Up, Thumbs Down (p. 71)

CLUES

2 syllables
cus/tom
hap/pen
o/ver
pa/per
wel/come

3 syllables
bi/cy/cle
re/la/tion
u/ni/corn

4 syllables
al/li/ga/tor
tel/e/vi/sion

5 syllables
bi/cen/ten/ni/al
hip/po/pot/a/mus

Watch Out!

beau	de/li/cious	ox/y/gen
beau/ty	fa/mous	rhy/thm
be/cause	gor/geous	suite
bur/eau	mosque	you
cyst	out/ra/geous	

SOLUTION

- A syllable is a portion of a word that contains exactly one vowel sound.
- Words have as many syllables as they do vowel sounds.
- A single vowel can be a syllable all by itself.

(Note: Be aware of the difference between a vowel and a vowel sound. Some vowel sounds are made by a combination of vowels, and, once in a while, a vowel sound is made without the presence of a vowel, as in *rhythm*.)

Here are a few Solution Stretchers you can use to extend the learning:

How are compound words and words with prefixes and suffixes divided into syllables?

DECODING MYSTERY
#17

CLUES

prefix	suffix
im/press	luck/less
mis/spoke	sure/ly
pre/cook	sweet/ness
re/make	tax/es

compound word

can/not
care/free
eye/sore
song/bird

Watch Out!

prel/ate	rel/a/tive
pri/ces	rep/re/sent

MINI-LESSONS

Here are a few you can use to teach this Language Mystery:

- Card Sort (p. 65)
- Computer Slideshow (p. 66)
- Field Detectives (p. 67)
- Hypothesize (p. 67)
- Secret Boxes (p. 70)

SOLUTION

- The syllable break in compound words comes between the two words that make up the compound.
- Words with prefixes usually have a syllable break right after the prefix.
- Words with suffixes usually have a syllable break right before the suffix.

Here are a few Solution Stretchers you can use to extend the learning:

Board Games (p. 73)

Kinesthetic Spelling (p. 80)

Pattern Campaign (p. 81)

Pattern Links (p. 82)

Pizza Slices (p. 83)

Reach for the Stars (p. 85)

Reference Books (p. 85)

Word Banks (p. 88)

How does the arrangement of consonants and vowels help divide words into syllables?

CLUES

2 consonants	1 consonant
ban/ner	mu/sic
can/dle	o/ver
hap/pen	pa/per
mis/ter	ta/ble

MINI-LESSONS

Here are a few you can use to teach this Language Mystery:

- Card Sort (p. 65)
- Field Detectives (p. 67)
- Hypothesize (p. 67)
- Secret Boxes (p. 70)
- Sound House (p. 71)

Watch Out!

li/sten	o/ften	tow/el
neigh/bor	roy/al	whi/stle

SOLUTION

- When two vowel sounds are separated by two consonants, the syllable break comes between the two consonants, even if those consonants are the same.
- When two vowel sounds are separated by one consonant, the syllable break comes before the consonant. The first vowel sound is usually long.

(Note: Remember that *w* and *y* often act as part of vowel sounds and not as independent consonants.)

Here are a few Solution Stretchers you can use to extend the learning:

Bouquets (p. 74)	Pattern Links (p. 82)
Discussion Session (p. 76)	Raining Rules (p. 84)
Dungeon Keeper (p. 77)	Single Elimination (p. 86)
Highlighter Hunt (p. 79)	Tic-Tac-Toe (p. 87)

How are vowels in words with more than one syllable pronounced?

CLUES

1st syllable open	1st syllable closed
a/corn	back/ward
cre/ate	ex/pend
i/de/a	in/vent
mo/ment	lof/ty
mu/sic	mus/tard
try/ing	sys/tem

Watch Out!

a/bout	e/rupt	hope/ful	mu/si/cian
a/lone	ha/bit	mea/sure	un/like/ly

MINI-LESSONS

Here are a few you can use to teach this Language Mystery:

- Card Sort (p. 65)
- Computer Slideshow (p. 66)
- Field Detectives (p. 67)
- Secret Boxes (p. 70)
- Sound House (p. 71)

SOLUTION

- When a vowel sound ends a syllable, it is usually long. This is called an open syllable.
- When a consonant sound ends a syllable, that syllable's vowel sound is usually short. This is called a closed syllable.

(Note: When a long-vowel sound is created by a vowel combination or the silent *e*, the above rules do not apply. Finding root words in longer words helps determine the pronunciation of the vowel sound.)

Here are a few Solution Stretchers you can use to extend the learning:

Cross the River (p. 76)

Fill the Basket (p. 77)

Flash Card Relay (p. 78)

Language Mysteries Notebook (p. 80)

Raining Rules (p. 84)

Reference Books (p. 85)

Single Elimination (p. 86)

Tic-Tac-Toe (p. 87)

Encoding Mysteries (Spelling)

Encoding Mysteries include patterns that students can apply when spelling words they know how to pronounce. For example, the pattern that tells whether the /k/ sound is spelled *c*, *k*, or *ck* at the end of a word appears in this section (Encoding Mystery #3). The term *encoding* is often used in reference to transferring words from oral language to written language.

This table shows which **Mini-Lessons** can be used to introduce each Encoding Mystery.

Encoding Mystery #	Around the Circle (p. 65)	Card Sort (p. 65)	Computer Slideshow (p. 66)	Does It Belong? (p. 66)	Field Detectives (p. 67)	Hypothesize (p. 67)	In My Bag (p. 68)	Name That Mystery (p. 68)	Open Forum (p. 69)	Phonetic Spelling (p. 69)	Riddles (p. 70)	Secret Boxes (p. 70)	Sound House (p. 71)	Thumbs Up, Thumbs Down (p. 71)	Word Sleuth (p. 71)
1	X		X	X	X		X	X	X	X	X	X	X	X	X
2	X	X	X	X	X	X	X	X	X	X	X	X	X	X	X
3	X	X	X	X	X	X	X	X	X	X	X	X	X	X	X
4	X	X	X	X	X	X	X	X	X	X	X	X	X	X	X
5	X	X	X	X	X	X	X	X	X	X	X	X	X	X	X
6	X	X	X	X	X	X	X	X		X		X	X	X	X
7	X	X	X	X	X	X	X	X	X	X		X	X	X	X
8	X	X	X	X	X	X	X	X	X	X		X	X	X	X
9	X	X	X	X	X	X	X	X	X	X	X	X	X	X	X
10	X	X	X	X	X	X	X	X	X	X		X	X	X	X
11	X	X	X	X	X	X	X	X	X	X		X	X	X	X
12	X	X	X		X	X	X	X		X		X	X	X	X
13	X	X	X		X	X	X	X		X		X	X	X	X
14	X	X	X	X	X		X	X	X	X		X	X	X	X
15	X		X	X	X		X	X		X	X	X	X	X	X

This table shows which **Solution Stretchers** can be used with each Encoding Mystery.

ENCODING MYSTERY #	Banners (p. 73)	Board Games (p. 73)	Bouquets (p. 74)	Buzz In (p.74)	Catching Words (p. 75)	Cross the River (p. 76)	Discussion Session (p. 76)	Dungeon Keeper (p.77)	Fill the Basket (p. 77)	Flap Cards (p.78)	Flash Card Relay (p. 78)	Highlighter Hunt (p.79)	Holdup (p.79)	Kinesthetic Spelling (p. 80)	Lang. Mysteries Notebook (p. 80)	Mystery Montage (p. 81)	Pattern Campaign (p. 81)	Pattern Links (p. 82)	Pattern or Exception? (p. 82)	Pizza Slices (p. 83)	Puzzlemania (p. 84)	Raining Rules (p. 84)	Reach for the Stars (p. 85)	Reference Books (p. 85)	Single Elimination (p. 86)	Squeeze Them In (p. 86)	Swat It! (p. 87)	Tic-Tac-Toe (p. 87)	The Way Out (p. 88)	Word Banks (p. 88)	Word Roots (p. 89)	Wordball (p. 89)
1	x	x			x	x	x	x	x	x	x	x		x	x	x	x	x	x		x	x	x	x	x	x		x	x	x	x	x
2	x	x	x	x	x	x	x	x	x	x	x	x	x	x	x	x	x	x	x	x	x	x	x	x	x	x	x	x	x	x	x	x
3	x	x	x	x	x	x	x	x	x	x	x	x	x	x	x	x	x	x	x	x	x	x	x	x	x		x	x	x	x	x	x
4	x	x	x	x	x	x	x	x	x	x	x	x	x	x	x	x	x	x	x	x	x	x	x	x	x	x	x	x	x	x	x	x
5	x	x	x	x		x	x	x	x	x	x	x	x	x	x	x	x	x	x	x	x	x	x	x	x	x	x	x	x	x	x	x
6	x	x	x	x	x	x	x	x	x	x	x	x	x	x	x	x	x	x	x		x	x	x	x	x	x	x	x	x	x	x	x
7	x	x	x	x	x	x	x	x	x	x	x	x	x	x	x	x	x	x	x	x	x	x	x	x	x	x	x	x	x	x	x	x
8	x	x	x	x	x	x	x	x	x	x	x	x	x	x	x	x	x	x	x	x	x	x	x	x	x	x	x	x	x	x	x	x
9	x	x	x	x	x	x	x	x	x	x	x	x	x	x	x	x	x	x	x	x	x	x	x	x	x	x	x	x	x	x	x	x
10	x	x	x	x	x	x	x	x	x	x	x	x	x	x	x	x	x	x	x		x	x	x	x	x	x	x	x	x	x	x	x
11	x	x	x	x	x	x	x	x	x	x	x	x	x	x	x	x	x	x	x	x	x	x	x	x	x	x	x	x	x	x	x	
12		x	x			x		x	x	x	x	x		x	x	x	x	x	x	x		x	x	x	x	x		x	x	x	x	x
13		x	x			x		x	x	x	x	x		x		x	x	x			x		x	x	x	x		x	x	x		x
14	x	x	x		x	x		x	x	x	x	x		x		x	x	x	x	x		x	x	x	x	x		x	x	x	x	x
15	x	x			x	x	x	x	x	x	x	x		x	x	x	x	x	x		x	x	x	x	x	x		x	x	x	x	x

What sound and spelling pattern can be identified with the letter *q*?

CLUES

acquire	qualify	quiz
aquarium	quarrel	quote
banquet	quarter	request
equal	queen	require
equipment	question	squad
liquid	quiet	square
quack	quiver	tranquil

MINI-LESSONS

Here are a few you can use to teach this Language Mystery:

- Around the Circle (p. 65)
- Does It Belong? (p. 66)
- Open Forum (p. 69)
- Riddles (p. 70)
- Thumbs Up, Thumbs Down (p. 71)

Watch Out!

antique	liquor	picturesque
grotesque	mosquito	plaque
Iraq	opaque	quay
lacquer	physique	queue

SOLUTION

- *Q* has no sound of its own. *Q* is almost always followed by *u*, no matter where it appears in a word.
- The letter *u* in the combination of *qu* does not act like a vowel. Instead, *qu* makes the /kw/ consonant blend sound.
- The letters *que* at the end of a word make the /k/ sound.

Here are a few Solution Stretchers you can use to extend the learning:

Banners (p. 73)

Discussion Session (p. 76)

Flash Card Relay (p. 78)

Kinesthetic Spelling (p. 80)

Pattern or Exception? (p. 82)

Puzzlemania (p. 84)

Squeeze Them In (p. 86)

Wordball (p. 89)

How is the /k/ sound spelled at the beginning or in the middle of words?

CLUES

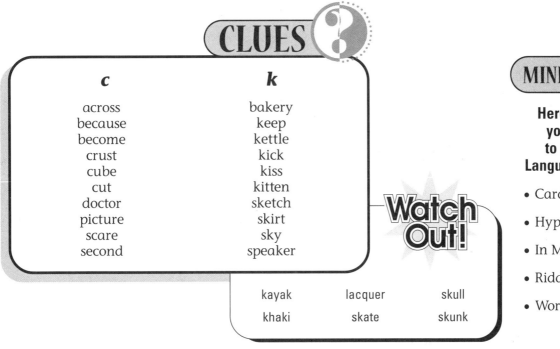

c	k
across	bakery
because	keep
become	kettle
crust	kick
cube	kiss
cut	kitten
doctor	sketch
picture	skirt
scare	sky
second	speaker

Watch Out!

kayak	lacquer	skull
khaki	skate	skunk

MINI-LESSONS

Here are a few you can use to teach this Language Mystery:

- Card Sort (p. 65)
- Hypothesize (p. 67)
- In My Bag (p. 68)
- Riddles (p. 70)
- Word Sleuth (p. 71)

SOLUTION

- Words in which the /k/ sound precedes *a, o, u,* or a consonant use *c.*
- Words in which the /k/ sound precedes *e, i,* or *y* use *k.*

Here are a few Solution Stretchers you can use to extend the learning:

Bouquets (p. 74)

Buzz In (p. 74)

Fill the Basket (p. 77)

Holdup (p. 79)

Pizza Slices (p. 83)

Puzzlemania (p. 84)

Swat It! (p. 87)

The Way Out (p. 88)

When are words ending in the /k/ sound spelled with *c, k,* or *ck?*

CLUES

c	k	ck
comic	beak	back
dramatic	hawk	block
electric	oak	deck
fantastic	peak	dock
music	pork	duck
panic	seek	kick
picnic	shark	lack
public	stark	neck
specific	stork	pick
topic	took	truck

Watch Out!

attack   shellac   tic   yak

maniac   stomach   wok

SOLUTION

- Polysyllabic words ending in /ĭk/ use *c.*
- One-syllable words that end in the /k/ sound and contain a vowel diphthong or digraph use *k.*
- One-syllable, short-vowel words ending in the /k/ sound use *ck.*

Here are a few Solution Stretchers you can use to extend the learning:

How is the /ch/ sound spelled at the end of a word?

CLUES

tch	ch
catch	approach
etch	branch
hatch	couch
itch	gulch
match	lunch
pitch	march
scratch	mulch
stretch	peach
switch	search
witch	slouch

Watch Out!

attach	much	sandwich	which
bachelor	rich	such	

MINI-LESSONS

Here are a few you can use to teach this Language Mystery:

- Computer Slideshow (p. 66)
- Does It Belong? (p. 66)
- Open Forum (p. 69)
- Sound House (p. 71)
- Thumbs Up, Thumbs Down (p. 71)

SOLUTION

- When the /ch/ sound follows a short-vowel sound, it is spelled *tch*.
- When the /ch/ sound follows any other sound, it is spelled *ch*.

Here are a few Solution Stretchers you can use to extend the learning:

Flap Cards (p. 78)

Highlighter Hunt (p. 79)

Language Mysteries Notebook (p. 80)

Pattern Campaign (p. 81)

Pattern or Exception? (p. 82)

Raining Rules (p. 84)

Single Elimination (p. 86)

Tic-Tac-Toe (p. 87)

ENCODING MYSTERY

#5

When are *ai* and *ay* used to spell the /ā/ sound? When are *oi* and *oy* used to spell the /oi/ sound?

MINI-LESSONS

Here are a few you can use to teach this Language Mystery:

- Around the Circle (p. 65)

- Card Sort (p. 65)

- Field Detectives (p. 67)

- Hypothesize (p. 67)

- Word Sleuth (p. 71)

❓ CLUES

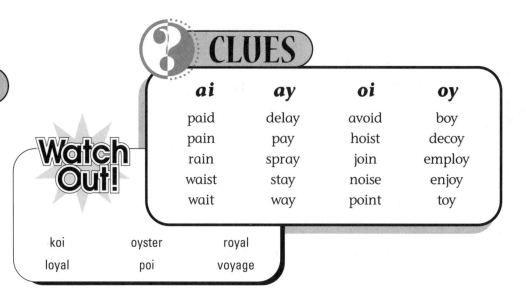

ai	*ay*	*oi*	*oy*
paid	delay	avoid	boy
pain	pay	hoist	decoy
rain	spray	join	employ
waist	stay	noise	enjoy
wait	way	point	toy

Watch Out!

koi	oyster	royal
loyal	poi	voyage

SOLUTION ❗

- Use *ai* to spell the /ā/ sound and *oi* to spell the /oi/ sound when the sound appears within the word.
- Use *ay* to spell the /ā/ sound and *oy* to spell the /oi/ sound when the sound appears at the end of a word.

Here are a few Solution Stretchers you can use to extend the learning:

Banners (p. 73)

Bouquets (p. 74)

Buzz In (p. 74)

Discussion Session (p. 76)

Flash Card Relay (p. 78)

Holdup (p. 79)

Swat It! (p. 87)

The Way Out (p. 88)

When are *s* and *es* used to make words plural?

ENCODING MYSTERY

#6

CLUES ?

add *es*	**add *s***
axes	barbers
brushes	encyclopedias
dresses	hurricanes
peaches	tests
quizzes	words
wishes	zebras

change *y* to *i*, add *es*

armies

centuries

juries

ladies

nurseries

pennies

Watch Out!

boys	rays
keys	stomachs

SOLUTION

- Add *es* to form the plural of words ending in *s, x, z, ch,* or *sh*.
- For words ending in a consonant + *y*, change the *y* to *i* and add *es*.
- Add *s* to form the plural of words ending in all other vowels and consonants.

MINI-LESSONS

Here are a few you can use to teach this Language Mystery:

- Computer Slideshow (p. 66)
- In My Bag (p. 68)
- Name That Mystery (p. 68)
- Phonetic Spelling (p. 69)
- Sound House (p. 71)

Here are a few Solution Stretchers you can use to extend the learning:

Board Games (p. 73)

Fill the Basket (p. 77)

Highlighter Hunt (p. 79)

Mystery Montage (p. 81)

Reference Books (p. 85)

Squeeze Them In (p. 86)

Word Banks (p. 88)

Word Roots (p. 89)

ENCODING MYSTERY #7

How does adding the suffixes -ing, -ed, and -er to words ending in y or w change their spelling?

CLUES

root ends in consonant + y	root ends in vowel + w or y
applying	destroying
hurrying	growing
marrying	playing
copied	clawed
emptied	delayed
tried	enjoyed
cloudier	drawer
earlier	employer
hungrier	mower

dryer	flyer
dyeing	fryer

MINI-LESSONS

Here are a few you can use to teach this Language Mystery:

- Around the Circle (p. 65)

- Does It Belong? (p. 66)

- Open Forum (p. 69)

- Secret Boxes (p. 70)

- Thumbs Up, Thumbs Down (p. 71)

SOLUTION

- For words ending with *y* following a consonant, add *-ing* without changing the spelling of the word. Change the *y* to *i* before adding *-ed* or *-er*.

- For words ending with *y* or *w* preceded by a vowel, add *-ing*, *-ed*, or *-er* without changing the spelling of the word.

Here are a few Solution Stretchers you can use to extend the learning:

Dungeon Keeper (p. 77)

Fill the Basket (p. 77)

Kinesthetic Spelling (p. 80)

Pattern Campaign (p. 81)

Pattern Links (p. 82)

Pizza Slices (p. 83)

Single Elimination (p. 86)

Tic-Tac-Toe (p. 87)

How does adding the suffixes -*ing*, -*ed*, and -*er* to long- and short-vowel words change their spelling?

CLUES

root ends in silent *e*	root ends in short vowel + consonant	others
baking	drumming	gulping
biking	sitting	jumping
braving	winning	raining
chased	jammed	clamped
dined	planned	roamed
hoped	ripped	waited
hiker	bigger	duster
stranger	chopper	painter
timer	robber	steamer

MINI-LESSONS

Here are a few you can use to teach this Language Mystery:

- Computer Slideshow (p. 66)
- Field Detectives (p. 67)
- In My Bag (p. 68)
- Sound House (p. 71)
- Word Sleuth (p. 71)

Watch Out!

boxed	boxing	mixer	singeing
boxer	mixed	mixing	

SOLUTION

- For words ending in silent *e*, drop the *e* before adding -*ing*, -*ed*, or -*er*.
- For words ending with one consonant following one short-vowel sound, double the consonant before adding -*ing*, -*ed*, or -*er*.
- For words with vowel combinations in the middle or consonant combinations at the end, add the suffix without changing the spelling.

Here are a few Solution Stretchers you can use to extend the learning:

#9

When is *-ar, -er,* or *-or* used at the end of a word?

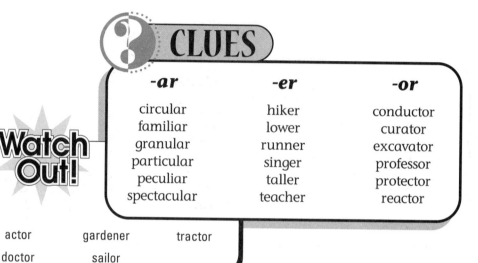

CLUES

-ar	-er	-or
circular	hiker	conductor
familiar	lower	curator
granular	runner	excavator
particular	singer	professor
peculiar	taller	protector
spectacular	teacher	reactor

Watch Out!

actor   gardener   tractor

doctor   sailor

MINI-LESSONS

Here are a few you can use to teach this Language Mystery:

- Card Sort (p. 65)
- Field Detectives (p. 67)
- Hypothesize (p. 67)
- Riddles (p. 70)
- Word Sleuth (p. 71)

SOLUTION

- Add *-ar* to words when the word is an adjective with more than two syllables.
- Add *-er* to one-syllable words when the suffix is a comparative or means "someone who" (e.g., a "worker" is someone who works). If the root word ends with a short vowel and a single consonant, double the consonant before adding *-er.*
- Add *-or* to polysyllabic words when the suffix means "someone who" (e.g., a "visitor" is someone who visits).

Here are a few Solution Stretchers you can use to extend the learning:

When is /shŭn/ at the end of a word spelled *sion* and when is it spelled *tion*?

CLUES

-*sion*	-*tion*
collision	accommodation
comprehension	action
compression	devotion
depression	dissection
discussion	emotion
expansion	execution
extension	fascination
recession	invention

Watch Out!

allegation	invitation
computation	redemption

MINI-LESSONS

Here are a few you can use to teach this Language Mystery:

- Computer Slideshow (p. 66)
- In My Bag (p. 68)
- Phonetic Spelling (p. 69)
- Sound House (p. 71)
- Thumbs Up, Thumbs Down (p. 71)

SOLUTION

- Add the suffix *-sion* when the root word ends in *d, de,* or *ss.* For root words ending in *d* or *de,* drop the *d* or *de* and add *-sion.* For root words ending in *ss,* add *-ion.*
- For root words ending in *t,* just add *-ion.* For root words ending in *te,* drop the *e* and add *-ion.*

(Note: When decoding *-sion* words, pronounce the suffix /shŭn/ when it follows a consonant. Pronounce it /zhŭn/ when it follows a vowel sound. This suffix means "the act or process of" and changes verbs ending in the /d/, /s/, and /t/ sounds to nouns. Other suffixes, such as *-ment, -al, -age,* and *-ism,* have the same function for words ending in other letters.)

Here are a few Solution Stretchers you can use to extend the learning:

Board Games (p. 73)

Buzz In (p. 74)

Discussion Session (p. 76)

Holdup (p. 79)

Reference Books (p. 85)

Swat It! (p. 87)

Word Roots (p. 89)

Wordball (p. 89)

When are the letters *ie* and *ei* used to spell words?

MINI-LESSONS

Here are a few you can use to teach this Language Mystery:

- Around the Circle (p. 65)
- Field Detectives (p. 67)
- Name That Mystery (p. 68)
- Open Forum (p. 69)
- Word Sleuth (p. 71)

CLUES

/ē/ = ie	/ē/ = ei	/ā/ = ei
believe	ceiling	beige
chief	conceit	freight
diesel	deceit	neighbor
fierce	deceive	reign
piece	perceive	reindeer
pier	receipt	veil
shield	receive	weigh

Watch Out!

foreign	friend	science	sieve	view
forfeit	height	seize	society	weird

SOLUTION

- When spelling the /ē/ sound, *i* comes before *e*, except when the sound follows the letter *c*. Then, it is spelled *ei*.
- When spelling the /ā/ sound, *e* comes before *i*.

(Note: A common rhyme used to remember this pattern is I *before* e, *except after* c, or *when sounded like* /ā/ *as in* neighbor *and* weigh.)

Here are a few Solution Stretchers you can use to extend the learning:

What vowels' sounds change when they precede an *l*? How are these vowels' sounds spelled?

CLUES

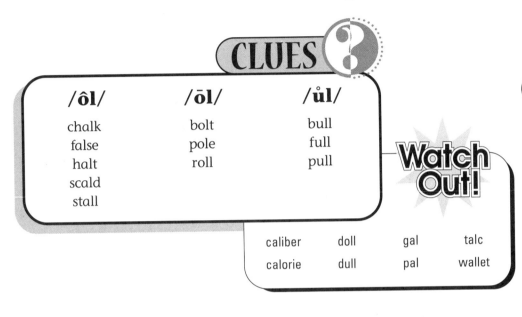

/ôl/	/ōl/	/ŭl/
chalk	bolt	bull
false	pole	full
halt	roll	pull
scald		
stall		

Watch Out!

caliber	doll	gal	talc
calorie	dull	pal	wallet

MINI-LESSONS

Here are a few you can use to teach this Language Mystery:

- Card Sort (p. 65)
- Hypothesize (p. 67)
- Phonetic Spelling (p. 69)
- Secret Boxes (p. 70)
- Sound House (p. 71)

SOLUTION

- The /ôl/ sound as in *ball* is usually spelled *al* in the middle of a word and *all* at the end of a word.
- The /ōl/ sound as in *roll* may be spelled *ol*, *oll*, or *ole*.
- The /ŭl/ sound as in *pull* is usually spelled *ull*.

(Note: Dialects may affect the pronunciation of *l*-controlled vowel sounds.)

Here are a few Solution Stretchers you can use to extend the learning:

Bouquets (p. 74)

Fill the Basket (p. 77)

Flash Card Relay (p. 78)

Language Mysteries Notebook (p. 80)

Pattern Campaign (p. 81)

Pattern or Exception? (p. 82)

Reach for the Stars (p. 85)

Single Elimination (p. 86)

ENCODING MYSTERY #13

What vowels' sounds change when they precede an *r*? How are these vowels' sounds spelled?

MINI-LESSONS

Here are a few you can use to teach this Language Mystery:

- Around the Circle (p. 65)
- Computer Slideshow (p. 66)
- Riddles (p. 70)
- Secret Boxes (p. 70)
- Word Sleuth (p. 71)

CLUES

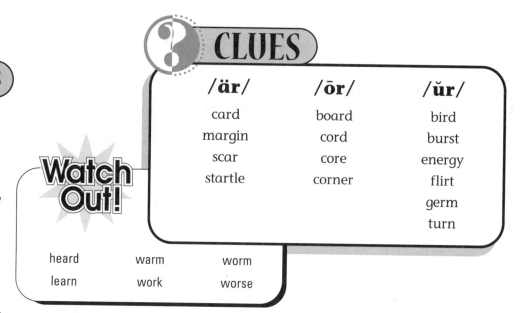

/är/	/ōr/	/ŭr/
card	board	bird
margin	cord	burst
scar	core	energy
startle	corner	flirt
		germ
		turn

Watch Out!

heard	warm	worm
learn	work	worse

SOLUTION

- The /är/ sound as in *are* is usually spelled *ar.*
- The /ōr/ sound as in *or* may be spelled *or, oar,* or *ore.*
- The /ŭr/ sound as in *her* may be spelled *er, ir,* or *ur.*

(Note: The long-vowel sounds of *a, e, i,* and *u* paired with *r* closely match their phonetic pronunciation. When *or* follows *w,* it has the /ŭr/ sound. Dialects may affect the pronunciation of *r*-controlled vowel sounds.)

Here are a few Solution Stretchers you can use to extend the learning:

Board Games (p. 73)

Cross the River (p. 76)

Dungeon Keeper (p. 77)

Flap Cards (p. 78)

Kinesthetic Spelling (p. 80)

Pattern Campaign (p. 81)

Pizza Slices (p. 83)

Raining Rules (p. 84)

What do the spellings of words ending in the /f/, /l/, and /s/ sounds have in common?

CLUES

short vowel + /f/, /l/, or /s/	long vowel + /f/, /l/, or /s/
bluff	beef
huff	leaf
staff	loaf
whiff	roof
ball	coal
dull	meal
skull	nail
wall	stool
boss	dose
dress	lease
hiss	loose
moss	vise

MINI-LESSONS

Here are a few you can use to teach this Language Mystery:

- Computer Slideshow (p. 66)
- Does It Belong? (p. 66)
- In My Bag (p. 68)
- Name That Mystery (p. 68)
- Thumbs Up, Thumbs Down (p. 71)

Watch Out!

deaf	has	if	scroll	troll
gas	helpful	pull	stroll	yes
gel	his	roll	toll	

SOLUTION

- *F, l,* and *s* are doubled at the end of most one-syllable, short-vowel words.
- One-syllable words containing long vowels, vowel digraphs, or vowel diphthongs use a single *f, l,* or *s.*

(Note: This pattern is often known as the "floss" pattern.)

Here are a few Solution Stretchers you can use to extend the learning:

Catching Words (p. 75)

Cross the River (p. 76)

Flap Cards (p. 78)

Kinesthetic Spelling (p. 80)

Mystery Montage (p. 81)

Raining Rules (p. 84)

Reference Books (p. 85)

Word Roots (p. 89)

How is the /ŭl/ sound at the end of a polysyllabic word spelled?

MINI-LESSONS

Here are a few you can use to teach this Language Mystery:

- Does It Belong? (p. 66)

- In My Bag (p. 68)

- Riddles (p. 70)

- Thumbs Up, Thumbs Down (p. 71)

- Word Sleuth (p. 71)

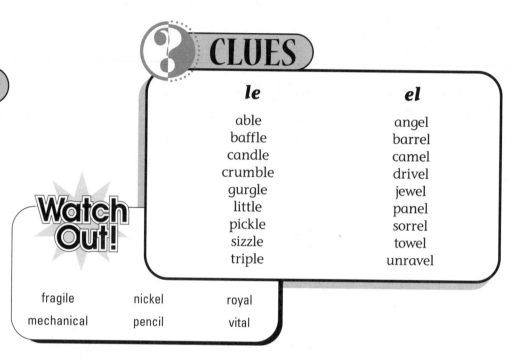

CLUES

le	el
able	angel
baffle	barrel
candle	camel
crumble	drivel
gurgle	jewel
little	panel
pickle	sorrel
sizzle	towel
triple	unravel

Watch Out!

fragile   nickel   royal

mechanical   pencil   vital

SOLUTION

- Words ending in the /ŭl/ sound preceded by /b/, /d/, /f/, /g/, /k/, /p/, /t/, and /z/ are spelled *le*.
- Words ending in the /ŭl/ sound preceded by /j/, /m/, /n/, /r/, /v/, *ew*, and *ow* are spelled *el*.

(Note: Words ending in the /ŭl/ sound preceded by a short vowel and the /s/ sound will be spelled *-ssel, -ssle,* or *-stle.*)

Here are a few Solution Stretchers you can use to extend the learning:

Banners (p. 73)

Catching Words (p. 75)

Cross the River (p. 76)

Fill the Basket (p. 77)

Flash Card Relay (p. 78)

Puzzlemania (p. 84)

Squeeze Them In (p. 86)

Wordball (p. 89)

Word-Solving Mysteries

(Comprehension and Vocabulary)

Word-Solving Mysteries include patterns that students can apply when deriving the meaning of unfamiliar words. For example, the pattern that tells which prefixes mean "not" or "the opposite of" appears in this section (Word-Solving Mystery #4). Word-Solving Mysteries are intended to help students expand their vocabulary and increase their comprehension skills.

This table shows which **Mini-Lessons** can be used to introduce each Word-Solving Mystery.

WORD-SOLVING MYSTERY #	Around the Circle (p. 65)	Card Sort (p. 65)	Computer Slideshow (p. 66)	Does It Belong? (p. 66)	Field Detectives (p. 67)	Hypothesize (p. 67)	In My Bag (p. 68)	Name That Mystery (p. 68)	Open Forum (p. 69)	Phonetic Spelling (p. 69)	Riddles (p. 70)	Secret Boxes (p. 70)	Sound House (p. 71)	Thumbs Up, Thumbs Down (p. 71)	Word Sleuth (p. 71)
1	x		x		x		x		x		x	x	x	x	x
2		x	x	x	x	x	x		x		x	x	x	x	x
3		x	x	x	x	x						x	x	x	
4	x		x	x	x	x	x	x	x		x	x	x	x	x
5	x	x	x	x	x	x			x			x	x	x	x
6	x	x	x	x	x	x	x	x	x			x	x	x	x
7			x	x	x	x						x	x	x	
8	x		x		x	x			x		x		x	x	x
9	x		x	x	x			x	x	x		x	x	x	x
10	x		x	x	x			x	x	x		x	x	x	x
11	x		x	x	x			x	x	x		x	x	x	x
12	x		x	x	x			x	x	x		x	x	x	x
13		x	x	x	x	x		x			x	x	x	x	x

This table shows which **Solution Stretchers** can be used with each Word-Solving Mystery.

Word-Solving Mystery #	Banners (p.73)	Board Games (p.73)	Bouquets (p.74)	Buzz In (p.74)	Catching Words (p.75)	Cross the River (p.76)	Discussion Session (p.76)	Dungeon Keeper (p.77)	Fill the Basket (p.77)	Flap Cards (p.78)	Flash Card Relay (p.78)	Highlighter Hunt (p.79)	Holdup (p.79)	Kinesthetic Spelling (p.80)	Lang. Mysteries Notebook (p.80)	Mystery Montage (p.81)	Pattern Campaign (p.81)	Pattern Links (p.82)	Pattern or Exception? (p.82)	Pizza Slices (p.83)	Puzzlemania (p.84)	Raining Rules (p.84)	Reach for the Stars (p.85)	Reference Books (p.85)	Single Elimination (p.86)	Squeeze Them In (p.86)	Swat It! (p.87)	Tic-Tac-Toe (p.87)	The Way Out (p.88)	Word Banks (p.88)	Word Roots (p.89)	Wordball (p.89)
1	x	x			x	x		x	x	x	x	x	x		x	x	x	x		x		x	x	x		x		x		x		x
2	x	x	x			x	x	x	x	x	x	x			x	x	x	x		x		x	x	x	x			x	x	x		x
3		x	x	x		x	x	x	x		x	x	x		x	x	x	x		x		x		x		x	x		x			
4	x	x	x		x	x	x	x	x	x	x	x		x	x	x	x	x	x	x	x	x	x	x	x	x		x	x	x	x	x
5		x			x	x	x	x	x	x	x	x		x	x	x	x	x	x	x	x	x		x	x	x		x	x	x		x
6	x	x	x		x	x	x	x	x	x	x	x		x	x	x	x	x		x		x	x	x	x	x		x	x	x	x	x
7		x	x	x		x	x	x	x		x	x	x	x	x	x	x	x		x		x		x	x	x	x	x	x	x		x
8		x	x		x	x	x	x	x	x	x	x			x	x	x	x	x		x	x		x		x		x	x	x	x	
9	x	x	x		x	x	x	x	x	x	x	x		x	x	x	x	x		x		x	x	x	x	x		x	x	x	x	x
10	x	x	x		x	x	x	x	x	x	x	x		x	x	x	x	x		x		x	x	x	x	x		x	x	x	x	x
11	x	x	x		x	x	x	x	x	x	x	x		x	x	x	x	x		x		x	x	x	x	x		x	x	x	x	x
12	x	x	x		x	x	x	x	x	x	x	x		x	x	x	x	x		x		x	x	x	x	x		x	x	x	x	x
13	x	x	x		x	x	x	x	x	x	x	x	x	x	x	x	x	x		x		x	x	x	x			x	x	x		

What does 's or s' mean when attached to the end of a word?

CLUES

boy's   girls'   teachers'   woman's

bus's   James's   Tom's   women's

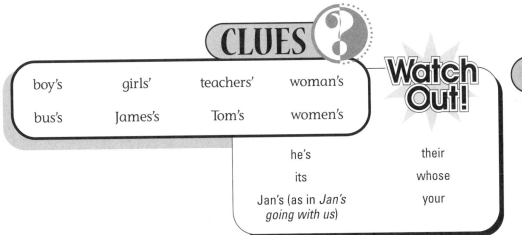

Watch Out!

he's   their

its   whose

Jan's (as in *Jan's going with us*)   your

MINI-LESSONS

Here are a few you can use to teach this Language Mystery:

- Around the Circle (p. 65)
- Field Detectives (p. 67)
- Open Forum (p. 69)
- Riddles (p. 70)
- Secret Boxes (p. 70)

SOLUTION

- An apostrophe before or after an *s* shows that something belongs to someone.
- For singular nouns and plural nouns that do not end in *s*, *'s* follows the word.
- For plural nouns ending in *s*, only an apostrophe is added.

(Note: Possessive forms of singular nouns ending in *s* are followed by *'s*. Possessive pronouns such as *its, whose, yours,* and *theirs* never have an apostrophe.)

Here are a few Solution Stretchers you can use to extend the learning:

Banners (p. 73)

Catching Words (p. 75)

Cross the River (p. 76)

Dungeon Keeper (p. 77)

Fill the Basket (p. 77)

Pattern Links (p. 82)

Reach for the Stars (p. 85)

Squeeze Them In (p. 86)

What does an apostrophe (') indicate in a word that is not a possessive?

MINI-LESSONS

Here are a few you can use to teach this Language Mystery:

- Card Sort (p. 65)
- In My Bag (p. 68)
- Open Forum (p. 69)
- Riddles (p. 70)
- Word Sleuth (p. 71)

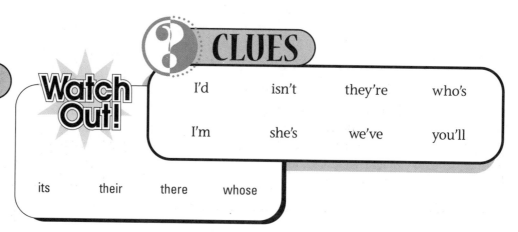

Watch Out!

? CLUES

| I'd | isn't | they're | who's |
| I'm | she's | we've | you'll |

its   their   there   whose

SOLUTION !

- An apostrophe may indicate two words have been put together into a contraction. It takes the place of missing letters. Contractions take on the meaning of the two words they incorporate.
- The following words are commonly used in contractions and have letters replaced by an apostrophe (the letters replaced are underlined): *am, are, have, is, not, will, would.*

(Note: Contractions are part of spoken language. They should be avoided in formal writing.)

Here are a few Solution Stretchers you can use to extend the learning:

Banners (p. 73)

Bouquets (p. 74)

Discussion Session (p. 76)

Flap Cards (p. 78)

Language Mysteries Notebook (p. 80)

Reach for the Stars (p. 85)

Single Elimination (p. 86)

The Way Out (p. 88)

What is the difference between pronouns like *who* and *whom, she* and *her,* and *he* and *him?*

CLUES

He sent the letter to John.
John sent the letter to him.
She saw Ruth.
Ruth saw her.
Who won first prize?
To whom was the trophy given?

Watch Out!

Tom is going with Jane and me.

Jane and I drove Tom and him to the store.

(These examples are correct, but they may seem awkward.)

MINI-LESSONS

Here are a few you can use to teach this Language Mystery:

- Card Sort (p. 65)
- Computer Slideshow (p. 66)
- Does It Belong? (p. 66)
- Sound House (p. 71)
- Thumbs Up, Thumbs Down (p. 71)

SOLUTION

- Some pronouns are used as the subject of a sentence—the doer of the action. These pronouns are *I, you, she, he, we, they,* and *who.*
- Some pronouns are used as the object of a sentence—the receiver of the action. These pronouns are *me, you, her, him, us, them,* and *whom.*

(Note: When a sentence has multiple subjects or objects, like those in the Watch Out! section, choose the pronoun by reading the sentence as if it had only the pronoun as the subject or object. For example, read *Tom is going with Jane and me* as *Tom is going with me* to find that *me* is the correct pronoun.)

Here are a few Solution Stretchers you can use to extend the learning:

Buzz In (p. 74)

Cross the River (p. 76)

Flash Card Relay (p. 78)

Holdup (p. 79)

Mystery Montage (p. 81)

Pizza Slices (p. 83)

Swat It! (p. 87)

Word Banks (p. 88)

What do the prefixes *a-, anti-, counter-, dis-, il-, im-, in-, ir-, mis-, non-,* and *un-* have in common?

CLUES

MINI-LESSONS

Here are a few you can use to teach this Language Mystery:

- Around the Circle (p. 65)
- In My Bag (p. 68)
- Open Forum (p. 69)
- Riddles (p. 70)
- Word Sleuth (p. 71)

Watch Out!

antiwar   illiterate   misconstrue
atypical   impersonal   nonsense
counteract   incorrect   uncertain
dishonest   irregular   unhappy

disturb   irritate   uniform
imply   mister   unsung

SOLUTION

- Each of these prefixes can mean "not" or "the opposite of."

(Note: A few other, less common prefixes have a similar meaning. For example, *mal-* and *dys-* mean "badly." The prefixes *im-* and *in-* can also mean "into.")

Here are a few Solution Stretchers you can use to extend the learning:

Catching Words (p. 75)

Flap Cards (p. 78)

Kinesthetic Spelling (p. 80)

Pattern or Exception? (p. 82)

Puzzlemania (p. 84)

Single Elimination (p. 86)

Squeeze Them In (p. 86)

The Way Out (p. 88)

What do the prefixes *pre-* and *re-* mean?

CLUES

pre-	re-
precaution	recall
precook	reheat
prefix	reinvent
preflight	rename
pregame	repay
pretest	reproduce

Watch Out!

pretend	redundant	reverse
pretense	renege	

MINI-LESSONS

Here are a few you can use to teach this Language Mystery:

- Card Sort (p. 65)
- Hypothesize (p. 67)
- Open Forum (p. 69)
- Secret Boxes (p. 70)
- Word Sleuth (p. 71)

SOLUTION

- *Pre-* in front of a root word means "before."
- *Re-* in front of a root word means "again."

Here are a few Solution Stretchers you can use to extend the learning:

Discussion Session (p. 76)

Pattern or Exception? (p. 82)

Pizza Slices (p. 83)

Puzzlemania (p. 84)

Raining Rules (p. 84)

Single Elimination (p. 86)

Tic-Tac-Toe (p. 87)

Wordball (p. 89)

What do the prefixes *em-*, *en-*, *im-*, and *in-* have in common? How do you know when to use each one?

CLUES

Watch Out!

em-	en-	im-	in-
embattle	enclose	imbalance	inactive
embrace	enlist	impartial	indecisive
empower	enraptured	impossible	injustice

emancipate   enmity   include

emergency   imagine   inhale

energy   imitate

MINI-LESSONS

Here are a few you can use to teach this Language Mystery:

- Computer Slideshow (p. 66)

- In My Bag (p. 68)

- Name That Mystery (p. 68)

- Thumbs Up, Thumbs Down (p. 71)

- Word Sleuth (p. 71)

SOLUTION

- The prefixes *em-* and *en-* both mean "bring in" or "bring to."
- The prefixes *im-* and *in-* usually mean "not" or "the opposite of." However, they sometimes can mean "into." Use the context of the sentence for clarification.
- Prefixes ending in *n* precede all vowel sounds and the sounds /d/, /f/, /g/, /h/, /j/, /k/, /l/, /r/, /s/, /t/, /v/, and /w/.
- Prefixes ending in *m* precede the sounds /b/, /m/, and /p/.

Here are a few Solution Stretchers you can use to extend the learning:

How do common prefixes affect word meanings?

CLUES

number
biweekly
quadrant
triangle
unicycle

location
interstate
intramural
midsection
submarine

negation
disbelief
impersonal
nonfiction
undo

time
afternoon
postwar
preheat

extent
extracurricular
multifunctional
outdistance
superhuman

Watch Out!

extravagant   multiply   unicorn

introduce   supervisor

SOLUTION

- Prefixes can be categorized by how they affect root words. Some of the most common prefix groups express the following:

  number (e.g., *bi-, quad-, tri-, uni-*)

  relative time (e.g., *after-, post-, pre-*)

  relative location (e.g., *inter-, intra-, mid-, sub-*)

  extent (e.g., *extra-, multi-, out-, super-*)

  negation (e.g., *dis-, im-/in-, non-, un-*)

(Note: Some words, such as those in the Watch Out! section, have prefixes but the root word does not help decipher the word's meaning. For example, *supervisor* does not mean "above a visor," but "above" is a clue toward discovering the word's meaning.)

MINI-LESSONS

Here are a few you can use to teach this Language Mystery:

- Card Sort (p. 65)
- Does It Belong? (p. 66)
- Field Detectives (p. 67)
- Hypothesize (p. 67)
- Sound House (p. 71)

Here are a few Solution Stretchers you can use to extend the learning:

How do the suffixes -er and -est change word meanings?

MINI-LESSONS

Here are a few you can use to teach this Language Mystery:

- Around the Circle (p. 65)
- Card Sort (p. 65)
- Computer Slideshow (p. 66)
- Open Forum (p. 69)
- Riddles (p. 70)

? CLUES

big, bigger, biggest   pretty, prettier, prettiest

deep, deeper, deepest   small, smaller, smallest

long, longer, longest   tame, tamer, tamest

Watch Out!

beautiful, more beautiful, most beautiful

good, better, best

little, less, least

much, more, most

SOLUTION !

- When attached to an adjective, the *-er* suffix indicates a comparison between exactly two things. The *-er* attached to the word indicates that the thing being described possesses more of that quality (e.g., lucky, ugly, lonely, tall) than something else.
- The *-est* suffix indicates a comparison between more than two things. The *-est* attached to a word indicates that it possesses more of that quality than all other things being compared to it.
- Adjectives with three or more syllables do not take the *-er* and *-est* endings. When used in comparisons, they are preceded by *more* or *most*.

(Note: The suffix *-er* can also mean "someone who" when attached to verbs. The comparative suffix *-er* can only be attached to adjectives.)

Here are a few Solution Stretchers you can use to extend the learning:

What do the suffixes -en, -ful, -less, -like, and -ous have in common?

 CLUES

-en
earthen
golden
wooden

-ful
beautiful
fearful
wonderful

-less
careless
fearless
thoughtless

-like
childlike
homelike
lifelike

-ous
humorous
joyous
luxurious

MINI-LESSONS

Here are a few you can use to teach this Language Mystery:

- Does It Belong? (p. 66)
- In My Bag (p. 68)
- Name That Mystery (p. 68)
- Thumbs Up, Thumbs Down (p. 71)
- Word Sleuth (p. 71)

Watch Out!

artful	cupful	misshapen
babyish	laborious	plentiful
beauteous	mischievous	

 SOLUTION

- Each suffix listed changes a noun into an adjective. The adjective created describes things in relation to the noun root word of the adjective. These suffixes are defined as follows:

  -en = made of   -like = relating/similar to
  -ful = full of   -ous = full of
  -less = without

(Note: If a root word ends in silent e, drop the e when adding a suffix that begins with a vowel [e.g., *proven*]. If a suffix begins with a consonant, keep the silent e at the end of the root word [e.g., *hopeful*]. If a root word ends in y preceded by a vowel, just add the suffix [e.g., *joyful*]. If it ends in y preceded by a consonant, change the y to i before adding a suffix that begins with a vowel [e.g., *luxurious*].)

Here are a few Solution Stretchers you can use to extend the learning:

Bouquets (p. 74)

Discussion Session (p. 76)

Flap Cards (p. 78)

Flash Card Relay (p. 78)

Kinesthetic Spelling (p. 80)

Reach for the Stars (p. 85)

Single Elimination (p. 86)

Tic-Tac-Toe (p. 87)

WORD-SOLVING MYSTERY

#10

What do the suffixes -*ant*, -*er*, -*ion*, and -*ment* have in common?

MINI-LESSONS

Here are a few you can use to teach this Language Mystery:

- Around the Circle (p. 65)
- Field Detectives (p. 67)
- Name That Mystery (p. 68)
- Sound House (p. 71)
- Thumbs Up, Thumbs Down (p. 71)

CLUES

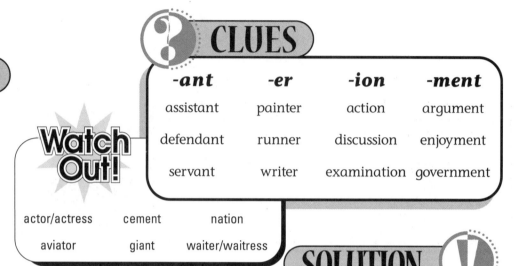

-*ant*	-*er*	-*ion*	-*ment*
assistant	painter	action	argument
defendant	runner	discussion	enjoyment
servant	writer	examination	government

Watch Out!

actor/actress   cement   nation

aviator   giant   waiter/waitress

SOLUTION

- Each suffix listed changes a verb into a noun. The noun created relates to the enacting of the verb. These suffixes are defined as follows:

-*ant* = one who	-*ion* = action or process
-*er* = one who	-*ment* = action or process

(Note: If a root word ends in silent *e*, drop the *e* when adding a suffix that begins with a vowel. If a suffix begins with a consonant, keep the silent *e* at the end of the root word unless the suffix is -*ion*. In that case, change the *e* to *at*, and then add the suffix [e.g., *invitation*]. If a root word ends in *y* preceded by a vowel, just add the suffix. If it ends in *y* preceded by a consonant, change the *y* to *i* before adding a suffix that begins with a vowel. The suffix -*or* is used in place of -*er* when the root word has more than one syllable. The suffix -*ess* may be used as a feminine form of -*er*.)

Here are a few Solution Stretchers you can use to extend the learning:

Banners (p. 73)

Catching Words (p. 75)

Fill the Basket (p. 77)

Highlighter Hunt (p. 79)

Pattern Links (p. 82)

Raining Rules (p. 84)

Reference Books (p. 85)

Wordball (p. 89)

What do the suffixes *-able/-ible, -(at)ive, -some,* and *-ed* have in common?

CLUES

-able/-ible
dependable
sensible
usable

-(at)ive
creative
relative
talkative

-some
awesome
meddlesome
tiresome

-ed
hurried
painted
rented

Watch Out!

handsome	manageable	peaceable
intelligible	native	soluble

MINI-LESSONS

Here are a few you can use to teach this Language Mystery:

- Around the Circle (p. 65)
- Computer Slideshow (p. 66)
- In My Bag (p. 68)
- Name That Mystery (p. 68)
- Secret Boxes (p. 70)

SOLUTION

- Each suffix listed changes a verb into an adjective. The adjective created describes a thing as something that does the action of the root verb. These suffixes are defined as follows:

  -able/-ible = capable of   *-some* = inclined to
  -(at)ive = inclined to   *-ed* = having the quality of

(Note: The suffixes *-able* and *-ible* are pronounced the same and have no patterns that indicate when one is used over the other. The suffix *-able* is more common. Adjectives with the suffix *-ed* can also be used as past-tense verbs. They are used as adjectives in phrases such as *a hurried throw, a painted wall,* and *a rented house.*)

Here are a few Solution Stretchers you can use to extend the learning:

Cross the River (p. 76)
Highlighter Hunt (p. 79)
Kinesthetic Spelling (p. 80)
Language Mysteries Notebook (p. 80)

Reach for the Stars (p. 85)
Reference Books (p. 85)
Word Banks (p. 88)
Word Roots (p. 89)

WORD-SOLVING MYSTERY #12

What do the suffixes *-ism*, *-ness*, *-sion*, and *-ty* have in common?

MINI-LESSONS

Here are a few you can use to teach this Language Mystery:

- Around the Circle (p. 65)

- Does It Belong? (p. 66)

- Field Detectives (p. 67)

- Open Forum (p. 69)

- Word Sleuth (p. 71)

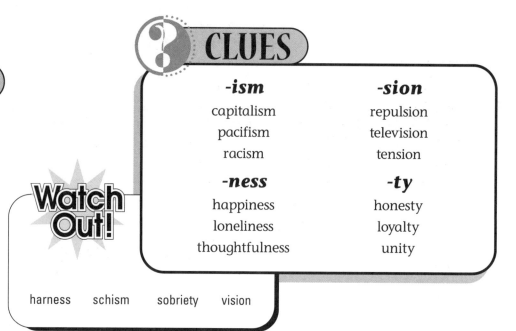

CLUES

-ism	*-sion*
capitalism	repulsion
pacifism	television
racism	tension

-ness	*-ty*
happiness	honesty
loneliness	loyalty
thoughtfulness	unity

Watch Out!

harness   schism   sobriety   vision

SOLUTION

- Each suffix listed changes an adjective into a noun and means "the quality or condition of."

(Note: The definition of a word with these suffixes may relate to its root word accompanied by another suffix. For example, *repulsion* means "the quality of being repul<u>sive</u>.")

Here are a few Solution Stretchers you can use to extend the learning:

Board Games (p. 73)

Dungeon Keeper (p. 77)

Flap Cards (p. 78)

Mystery Montage (p. 81)

Raining Rules (p. 84)

Squeeze Them In (p. 86)

The Way Out (p. 88)

Wordball (p. 89)

How can parts of a word give clues about the whole word's meaning?

CLUES

auto	graph	scope
autograph	graphic	microscope
automatic	phonograph	periscope
automobile	telegraph	telescope
bio	**mid**	**sign**
antibiotic	amid	insignia
biology	middle	sign
bionic	midnight	signature
geo	**ped**	**tele**
geography	centipede	telepathy
geologist	pedal	telephone
geometry	pedestrian	television

Watch Out!

autopsy	microscopic	timid
graphite	peddle	

MINI-LESSONS

Here are a few you can use to teach this Language Mystery:

- Card Sort (p. 65)
- Hypothesize (p. 67)
- Riddles (p. 70)
- Secret Boxes (p. 70)
- Sound House (p. 71)

SOLUTION

- Many English words include word parts based on words from other languages, frequently Latin and Greek. Knowing the meaning of these word parts can provide important clues to understanding new words. Some common word parts are

aqua = water (Latin)	*dent* = teeth (Latin)	*meter* = measure (Greek)	*phono* = sound (Greek)
astro = star (Greek)	*geo* = earth (Greek)	*mid* = middle (Latin)	*photo* = light (Greek)
auto = self (Greek)	*grad* = step (Latin)	*mobile* = moving (Latin)	*scop* = look (Greek)
bio = life (Greek)	*graph* = to write (Greek)	*morph* = shape (Greek)	*scribe* = write (Latin)
chron = time (Greek)	*lab* = work (Latin)	*mort* = death (Latin)	*sign* = mark (Latin)
cogn = know (Latin)	*logy* = study of (Greek)	*nat* = born (Latin)	*tele* = far (Greek)
cycle = circle (Greek)	*man* = hand (Latin)	*ped* = foot (Latin)	*terr* = land (Latin)

Here are a few Solution Stretchers you can use to extend the learning:

Discussion Session (p. 76)

Fill the Basket (p. 77)

Flash Card Relay (p. 78)

Holdup (p. 79)

Kinesthetic Spelling (p. 80)

Pattern Campaign (p. 81)

Reach for the Stars (p. 85)

Single Elimination (p. 86)

Mini-Lessons

This section contains 15 ideas for presenting Language Mysteries. These ideas are adaptable to many Language Mysteries and afford you a great deal of flexibility. If your students particularly enjoy one Mini-Lesson format, use it to present several Language Mysteries. If your students struggle with a Mystery presented in one format, reteach the Mystery in a different format until they grasp the language pattern. These activities are intended to take 10–20 minutes and provide an introduction to a language pattern.

Around the Circle

Write Clues words on index cards. Make enough for each student to have a card, even if more than one student has the same word. Give each student a card, and divide the class into two groups. (Join one of the groups if you have an odd number of students.) Have one group sit in a circle and the other group sit in a circle inside the first group's circle, facing the students in the first group. Ask students to compare their word with the person they are facing and discuss what the words have and do not have in common. Invite them to take notes on the back of their card. After an appropriate amount of time, have the outer circle rotate clockwise, giving each student a new partner. Again, have students compare words and discuss similarities. Continue until the outer circle has rotated completely and students are back with their original partner. At this point, discuss as a class the similarities between the words and generate the Solution to the Language Mystery. Challenge students to brainstorm other words to add to the Clues and Watch Out! lists.

Card Sort

Prepare several identical sets of index cards containing Clues words. Divide the class into groups, and give each group a set of cards. Ask the groups to sort the cards based on any criteria they choose. (You may wish to tell them how many sets of cards they should create.) Then, invite groups to share how they sorted their cards. If a group sorts their cards according to the correct pattern, identify the pattern, and, as a class, create a list of words that fit the pattern.

music
picnic
topic

beak
shark
took

deck
kick
truck

U se a slideshow program to create a series of slides featuring Clues words that fit a language pattern. List the Language Mystery on the first slide. After the Clues slides, create a slide for Watch Out! words. Introduce this slideshow at the beginning of the week. Over the course of the week, invite students to work with the slideshow independently or in pairs and write out and turn in hypotheses that explain the pattern. At the end of the week, or after all students have worked with the slideshow, discuss as a class the actual Solution to the Mystery. Invite students to use their free time to create additional slides for the show, and make the slideshow available for student reference.

Computer Slideshow

W rite on each of several large index cards three words that fit a language pattern and one that does not. For Mysteries whose Solution has multiple conditions, such as using *ay* versus *ai*, list three words that fit one condition and one that fits another (e.g., *play, tray, stay, rain*). For Mysteries with only one condition in their Solution, such as doubling *f, l,* and *s* at the end of one-syllable words, include three Clues words and one Watch Out! word (e.g., *miss, puff, will, bus*). Divide the class into groups, and give each group a card. Challenge the groups to determine which word does not belong with the others and create a hypothesis that explains their answer. Invite each group to present their hypothesis to the class, and guide the class to a consensus on the language pattern.

Does It Belong?

Field Detectives

Select three or four Language Mysteries to cover. Create a composite list of Clues words for all of the Mysteries. Divide the class into groups of four or five students. Give each group a Language Mystery question and a copy of the composite list of Clues words. Challenge groups to identify Clues words that apply to their Mystery and formulate an explanation of the pattern. To fit this activity into a mini-lesson format, divide the assignment among several days. For example, assign the Mysteries on Monday, have groups meet on Tuesday, and have groups present their explanations to the class Wednesday through Friday. As a whole class, check and discuss the groups' findings. Once the findings are verified by the class, reconvene the groups. Have each group make a poster of their findings. Display the posters in class.

Hypothesize

Prepare index cards containing Clues words. Use poster putty to attach them to the outer edges of a chalkboard or white board. Divide the board into sections labeled *A*, *B*, and *C* (or use the number of letters equal to the conditions of the Mystery's Solution). Place one word card in each section to set an example for students. Then, invite student volunteers to select a word card and place it in the section containing words that fit the same language pattern. Continue until all words are placed, and discuss why words fit in particular sections. Guide students to see patterns and create a hypothesis that explains each pattern. To allow more students to actively participate, break the class into groups and have each group formulate a hypothesis.

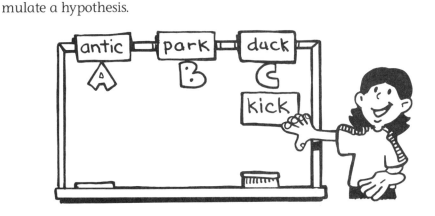

In My Bag

Hold up a large bag, and tell students that only words following a secret pattern can go in your bag. Their task will be to identify the pattern. List two or three Clues words and two or three Watch Out! words by saying *The words _____ and _____ can go in my bag, but _____ and _____ cannot.* Challenge students to think of words that might fit the secret pattern and ask you if those words can go in your bag. (You may need to suggest words that can go in your bag to keep the activity moving.) Invite students who think they can identify the pattern to guess what it is. When the class has correctly identified the pattern, write it on the board, discuss words named during the game that fit the pattern, and create a list of those words and others that also fit the pattern.

Name That Mystery

Divide the class into two teams, and assign each team a captain. Read a Clues word to the first team, and write it on the chalkboard. Ask the captain to declare how many more words his or her team needs to identify the pattern by saying *We can solve that Mystery with _____ clues!* Invite the captain of the other team to declare that they can solve the Mystery using fewer words or to challenge the first team to *Solve that Mystery.* When one team has been conceded to by the other, read and/or write the appropriate number of Clues words. Give the team 30 seconds to discuss what they think the pattern is and present their guess. If their guess is correct, write it on the board and give that team one point. If their guess is incorrect, give the other team a point and an opportunity to solve the Mystery for another point. If neither team can solve the Mystery, repeat the game, allowing teams to declare how many more words they need. After the Mystery has been solved, repeat the game during the same lesson or during following lessons with new captains. Keep an ongoing tally of teams' points, and award the winning team a prize or special privilege.

Open Forum

Write a Language Mystery question on the chalkboard or overhead projector, and invite students to suggest answers to the question. If they are unable to answer the question correctly, write a list of Clues words and a list of Watch Out! words. Tell students that the Clues words should help them answer the question because those words follow the pattern, while the Watch Out! words seem like they should, but do not. Invite students to participate in an open-forum discussion of the topic by suggesting words to add to either list, asking questions about the Mystery, and suggesting possible explanations of the pattern. You may wish to select students to serve as the mediator (person who calls on others to contribute) and recorder (person who writes down comments, questions, and suggestions). When students have arrived at the answer to the Mystery, brainstorm other words that fit in the Clues and Watch Out! lists.

Phonetic Spelling

Write on the chalkboard or overhead projector the phonetic spellings of Clues words from the Language Mystery. Leave room next to each word for the word to be written properly. Ask students to pronounce each word, and invite them to suggest the actual spelling of the words. Write the correct spelling next to the phonetic spelling. After writing the correct spelling for each word, discuss patterns students see and hear in the words. Guide them to discover the Solution to the Language Mystery.

Riddles

Turn a Language Mystery into a riddle by rephrasing its Solution and giving Clues and Watch Out! words as examples. For instance, give students clues such as *I can make short vowels long. I come at the end of a word. I may lose my power if I follow two consonants. Who am I?* (Silent *e*) Invite students to guess after each clue until the answer is revealed. Close the lesson by challenging the class to list as many words as possible that follow that language pattern.

Secret Boxes

Collect shoe boxes so you have one for each condition of a Language Mystery's Solution, and label each box with a sample word that fits one of the pattern's conditions. If the Mystery's Solution has only one condition, obtain two boxes—one for words that fit the pattern and one for words that do not. Write on index cards Clues words from the language pattern, one word per card. (For one-condition patterns, create some word cards that fit the pattern and some that do not.) During a break that precedes quiet, independent work time (or before the school day begins), place a card on each student's desk. Without discussing the language pattern, challenge students to place their card in the correct box. During the next day's lesson, list on the chalkboard or overhead projector the words from each box. Challenge students to find a pattern within the words and decide if any words were placed in the wrong box. Close the lesson by restating the pattern and placing the cards from the boxes on a word wall for future reference.

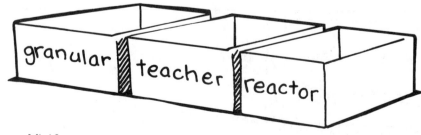

Draw an outline of a house on the chalkboard. This is the "sound house." Ask students a Language Mystery question, and suggest a few words that fit the pattern or a condition of the pattern. Write these words inside the house outline. Challenge students to suggest other words that can be "admitted" to the sound house. Ask students who suggest an appropriate word to write the word inside the house. Invite students to scan through curriculum materials, library books, or other easily accessible resources to find words. For Language Mysteries whose Solution has multiple conditions, draw one house outline for each condition and have students write words that fit the pattern in the appropriate house.

Open the lesson by posing the Language Mystery question and its Solution. Say aloud several Clues words, Watch Out! words, and other words. Ask students to show thumbs up if the word you say follows the language pattern and thumbs down if it does not. For Mysteries whose Solution has multiple conditions, such as using *ay* versus *ai*, write and number the options on the board. Instead of showing thumbs up or thumbs down, ask students to hold up the number of fingers corresponding with the number of the correct condition. For example, if *ai* is labeled *2* and you say *plain*, students should hold up two fingers. After reviewing several words, invite student volunteers to restate the Language Mystery and its Solution.

List on the chalkboard Clues for a Language Mystery, but use blank lines to replace the letters that identify the pattern. Challenge students to work independently, in pairs, or in small groups to deduce what letter or group of letters can be placed in each set of blank lines to create a real word. Invite students to suggest answers, and when the correct answer has been given, discuss the language pattern. Close the lesson by inviting students to suggest other words that fit the pattern.

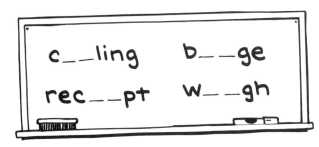

Solution Stretchers

This section contains 32 independent, small-group, whole-group, and learning-center extension activities you can use to provide further practice with language patterns you introduced through Mini-Lessons. Like the Mini-Lessons, these activities are adaptable to many different Language Mysteries. Unlike the Mini-Lessons, these activities are intended to fill larger amounts of time and reinforce, rather than introduce, the application of language patterns covered earlier.

D ivide the class into groups, and assign each group a Language Mystery. Have the groups cut and decorate butcher paper to create a banner in a shape that symbolizes their pattern. For example, a group working with the prefix *auto-* could create a car-shaped banner, and a group working with the "sounds of *y*" pattern could create a banner in the shape of a *y*. Invite groups to use markers or paint to write Clues words on their banner. Display finished banners around the room for student reference during writing activities.

Banners

MATERIALS

✓ scissors

✓ butcher paper

✓ markers or paint and paintbrushes

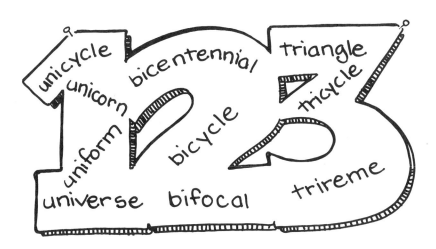

D ivide the class into groups. Assign each group a Language Mystery already covered in class. Have the groups use markers and poster board to design a board game that reviews and reinforces Clues and Watch Out! words from their Language Mystery. Remind them of qualities of an effective board game, such as clear rules, fun obstacles, and a brisk pace. Invite each group to present their game's rules and format to the entire class. Place the games at a learning center, and provide time for students to play all of the games.

Board Games

MATERIALS

✓ markers

✓ poster board

✓ dice

✓ game pieces

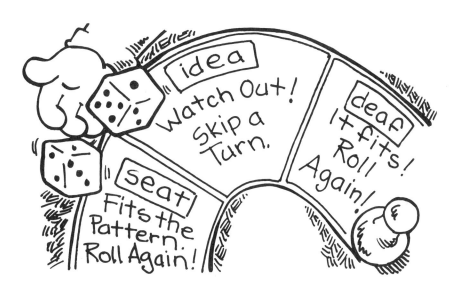

Divide the class into groups. Size the groups so the number of students in each group equals the number of conditions in the Solution of the Language Mystery. Give each student a sheet of construction paper and several die-cut flowers. Have students fold their paper in half and cut half of a flower vase shape beginning at the fold. Ask students to unfold their vase. Have students write a condition from the Language Mystery Solution on their vase so each group has one vase for each condition. Then, have students pool their die-cut flowers and write a word from one of the conditions on each flower. Finally, ask groups to glue a green pipe-cleaner stem to each flower and glue the stems to the matching vases. Display the "bouquets" on a bulletin board or around the room so students can refer to them later on.

Bouquets

MATERIALS

✓ construction paper

✓ die-cut flowers

✓ scissors

✓ glue

✓ green pipe cleaners

Choose a Language Mystery whose Solution has two or more conditions. Write these conditions on the chalkboard, and number each one. Divide the class into teams, and have each team line up single file behind a bell or buzzer. (The more teams you create, the more frequently students will participate.) Tell the teams that you will call out and/or write a Clues word, and the first player in each line must decide into which condition the word fits. The first player to ring the bell or buzzer, get called on, and answer correctly earns a point for his or her team. Say a Clues word, and call on the first player to ring in. Allow only a few seconds for the player to answer. If the player answers correctly, award his or her team a point. If not, give the other teams' players an opportunity to answer. Have the first player from each team go to the back of the line after the answer is announced. Play at least until all students have had a turn at the bell or buzzer. Reward the winning team with a privilege or small prize.

Buzz In

MATERIALS

✓ bells or buzzers

G ive each student a paper square, and have him or her follow these steps to create a "word catcher":

MATERIALS

✓ 8 ½" (21.5 cm) paper squares

1. Fold one corner across to the other corner to form a diagonal. Open the paper up again.

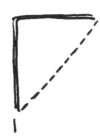

2. Repeat Step 1 for the opposite corners.

3. Fold each corner in to touch the center point.

4. Flip the paper over, and fold the corners again to touch the center point.

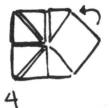

5. Create creases by folding the paper horizontally and vertically, opening it after each fold.

6. Bring the four corners together, and hold the corners under the flaps using thumbs and pointer fingers. The word catcher can be opened horizontally and vertically.

Ask students to open their catcher so it resembles Step 4. Have them write several Clues words for Language Mysteries on each of the eight triangles formed by the folds. Have them lift the flaps and write matching language patterns on the paper under the Clues words. Invite students to exchange their word catcher with a partner, open the word catcher horizontally and vertically, read the Clues words written on one of the flaps, and guess the language pattern the words identify. Have students check their answers by lifting the flaps.

C reate an 8 x 6 grid on tagboard. Write in each box a word that illustrates one of six Language Mysteries being reinforced. Place the words in the boxes randomly, but be sure the first column of six spaces contains one word from each Mystery. Write the six mysteries on drawing paper, and number them 1–6. Players each place a game piece at one end of the grid. They roll a die, find the Mystery that corresponds with the number they rolled, and move their game piece to a space in the first row containing a word that fits the pattern they rolled. Players take turns rolling the die and moving their game pieces, but they may only move their game pieces to adjacent squares. If the spaces around their piece do not contain an example of the pattern they rolled, they lose their turn. The first player to "cross the river" to the other side of the grid wins.

1. sounds of y
2. silent e
3. suffixes verb → noun
4. ch or tch
5. qu
6. /el/

G ive each student a list of Clues words for a Language Mystery the class recently solved. Have students read the list and think of a memorable way to recognize the pronunciation, spelling, and/or meaning of each word. For example, a student might say *I remember the silent g in sign because* signature *has the g sound.* Then, assign students partners or place them in groups, and have them discuss the memory cues they created. Have them decide on the most effective cue for each word by selecting one of the student's ideas or by creating a new idea. Ask students to write out these cues and present them to the class. As each pair or group presents their cues, invite the rest of the class to write down the ones they think will be helpful. This metacognition (thinking about one's thinking) is an excellent way for students to attach personal meaning to language patterns.

Cross the River

MATERIALS

✓ tagboard

✓ drawing paper

✓ game pieces (e.g., poker chips, dried beans)

✓ six-sided die

Discussion Session

MATERIALS

✓ lists of Clues words

Dungeon Keeper

MATERIALS

✓ index cards (optional)

✓ 4 pylons

Write a Language Mystery on each of several index cards. Take the class to the playground or gymnasium, and use four pylons to designate a "dungeon" area. You will act as the "dungeon keeper," standing near the pylons and holding the Language Mystery cards. Select two students to be "it" for a game of tag. When a student is tagged, "it" escorts him or her to the dungeon. In order to escape the dungeon, the student must draw a Language Mystery card and tell you a word that fits the pattern. (Note: Cards are not necessary if you choose to reinforce only one Language Mystery during the game.) Pause periodically to change students who are "it."

Fill the Basket

MATERIALS

✓ index cards

✓ baskets

Write on index cards Clues words from several Language Mysteries or from one Mystery whose Solution has several conditions. Write one word on each card. Mix up the cards, and pass out several cards to each student at random. Ask students to display the cards faceup on their desk. Choose students to be "collectors," and give each collector a basket. You should have one collector for each pattern. Assign each collector a pattern, and give the collectors a time limit to fill their basket with as many cards that fit their pattern as they can. Depending on your tolerance for noise, invite students at their desks to raise their hands, call out, or confer with collectors about which cards to place in their basket. At the end of the time limit, review each collector's pattern and the cards he or she collected. Discuss why each word follows the pattern. For each correct choice, award the collector one point. Repeat the game with new collectors and new patterns. This is an excellent contrast strategy for easily confused patterns, such as comparison suffixes and irregulars, *oi* and *oy*, and *ie* and *ei*.

Have students write on index cards Clues words from a Language Mystery, one word per card. Have them cut pieces of other index cards to cover the part of the word that is the focus of the Language Mystery and tape the cover to the top of the word card to create a flap. Invite students to use the flap cards to quiz themselves or their classmates on the identity of the words and the pattern. Have them check their answers by raising the flap.

Flap Cards

MATERIALS

✓ index cards

✓ scissors

✓ masking tape

Write Clues words for several Language Mysteries on index cards, one word per card. (You can also use a single Language Mystery whose Solution has several conditions.) Label a box for each pattern. Divide the class into two teams, and have the teams line up single file. Place the boxes an equal distance in front of each line. Place a stack of cards on a table at the front of each line. Upon a start signal, have the first student in each line take the top card off the team's pile, read the word on the card, place it in the correct container, and tag the next person in line. Then, that player draws a card and repeats the procedure. The first team to cycle through all its players is the winner. Monitor students to be sure they place the cards in the correct boxes. After the game is over, check the cards in each box and discuss how the words fit the patterns.

Flash Card Relay

MATERIALS

✓ index cards

✓ boxes

istribute newspapers and magazines to students. Give each student a highlighter pen, and have students search for and highlight words that fit a given Language Mystery. Have students use their findings to create a chart to share with the class, or create a chart together as a class. Conduct this activity in class, or have students use their materials to complete the assignment at home.

Highlighter Hunt

MATERIALS

✓ old newspapers and magazines

✓ highlighter pens

rite on large index cards Clues words for the Language Mystery students are working with. Give each student one blank index card for each condition of the Mystery's Solution. For example, if you are working with the "sounds of *y*" pattern, give each student four index cards. Discuss with students the conditions of the Solution, and have them write one on each of their cards. Be sure all students use the same wording for each condition. Hold up one of the Clues word cards (or call out the word), and challenge students to hold up the Solution card that matches the word as quickly as they can. Invite students who hold up the wrong card to correct their error. When students are all holding the correct card, have them put the card down and repeat the game. Play until all Clues words have been covered or until students clearly understand the language pattern.

Holdup

MATERIALS

✓ large index cards

ivide the class into groups. Be sure each group has at least as many members as the Language Mystery's longest Clues word has letters. Give each group a stack of drawing paper, and have the groups write each letter of the alphabet as large as possible on a sheet of paper. If your Clues words contain double letters, have groups make multiple sets of letters. Have the groups place their letter cards faceup in front of them. Call out a Clues word, and challenge the groups to pick up the letters that spell the word and arrange themselves in proper order. (In order for you to read the word, students will have to spell the word from their right to their left.) Award a point to the first group to finish. For bonus points, have groups divide themselves into syllables. Reward the team with the most points with a privilege or small prize.

Kinesthetic Spelling

MATERIALS

✓ drawing paper

ive each student a spiral-bound notebook (or ask students to bring one in), and have students number the upper right-hand corner of each page. As you present a Language Mystery and its Solution, have students add Clues and Watch Out! words to the notebook, one page per Mystery. Have students create a table of contents on the inside front cover of their notebook so they can refer to appropriate pages during their everyday reading and writing. Invite students to add to their notebook pages anytime they find an appropriate word.

Language Mysteries Notebook

MATERIALS

✓ spiral-bound notebooks

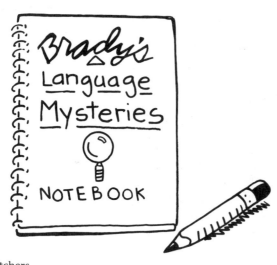

Divide the class into groups, and give each group a piece of poster board and a stack of old magazines, newspapers, and print ads. Challenge students to find, cut out, and glue to the poster board pictures or words that match the Solution to a Language Mystery. (Have each group work with the same Mystery, or assign each group their own Mystery.) Give students a time limit (20 minutes or so) in which to assemble their montage. Reward the group that fills their poster board first or most with a privilege or small prize. Write each Mystery's Solution on a sentence strip, and display the strips with the posters on a bulletin board for reference and decoration.

Mystery Montage

MATERIALS

✓ poster board

✓ old magazines, newspapers, and print ads

✓ scissors

✓ glue

✓ sentence strips

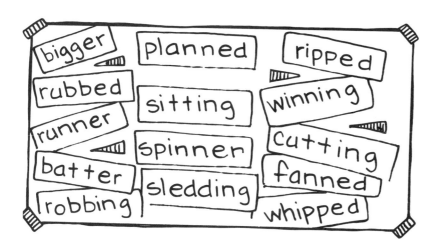

Divide the class into groups, and have each group determine which Language Mystery they think is most important for their classmates to know. Have groups use poster board and markers or paint to create campaign posters to convince their classmates of the importance of this language pattern. This activity can either be done like an advertising campaign where students spread the word about their pattern or like an election campaign where students eventually vote for the "Official Language Pattern of Room _____."

Pattern Campaign

MATERIALS

✓ poster board

✓ markers or paint and paintbrushes

Divide the class into groups, and assign each group a Language Mystery. Give each group a stack of construction paper strips and transparent tape. Invite the groups to write a Clues word from their Mystery on the center of each strip and create a chain by looping the strips into interlocking circles and taping them together. (For Mysteries whose Solution has multiple conditions, have students make a chain for each condition.) Ask the groups to write a description of their pattern on a sentence strip. Use pushpins to hang the chains and matching sentence strips on a bulletin board titled *Language Patterns: Links in a Chain.*

Pattern Links

MATERIALS

✓ construction paper strips

✓ transparent tape

✓ markers

✓ sentence strips

✓ pushpins

Divide the class into two teams. Tell the teams which Language Mystery you will be covering, and give them time to discuss and list Clues and Watch Out! words for that pattern. Then, have the teams line up facing each other. Call out either *Pattern* or *Exception* to the first person on one team. If that student successfully provides an example of the type of word asked for, he or she remains in the game. If not, he or she returns to his or her desk. Repeat the procedure for each student, alternating between the two teams. The team with the last player standing is the winner. (Most Language Mysteries have far more Clues words than Watch Out! words, so be sure the frequency with which you ask for pattern words or exceptions takes this into account.) Decide in advance whether or not students must name words no one prior to them used.

Pattern or Exception?

MATERIALS

✓ none

G ive students two butcher paper circles each. Have them draw light pencil lines on the circles so that each circle has one wedge for each condition of a Language Mystery's Solution. For example, the Solution to the "sounds of *y*" Mystery has four conditions, so students would divide each circle into four equal wedges. Have them cut out and discard a wedge from one of the circles.

Invite the class to suggest a pizza topping to represent each condition of the Solution. Using the "sounds of *y*" example, students may suggest pepperoni for the /ī/ sound, olives for the /ē/ sound, mushrooms for the /ĭ/ sound, and tomatoes for the /y/ consonant sound. Invite them to use construction paper scraps to create the pizza toppings they suggested. Ask students to write the Solution on the circle with the discarded wedge, write each condition on a matching topping, and glue the toppings to the circle. Invite students to write Clues words on appropriate toppings and fill each of the second circle's wedges with one type of topping. Finally, have students use a brass fastener to attach the circle with the discarded wedge on top of the Clues words circle. Create an interactive display by attaching the bottom circles to a bulletin board. Students can turn the top circles to find examples of each condition of the pattern's Solution.

Pizza Slices

MATERIALS

- ✓ 16" (40.5 cm) diameter butcher paper circles
- ✓ scissors
- ✓ construction paper scraps
- ✓ markers
- ✓ brass fasteners

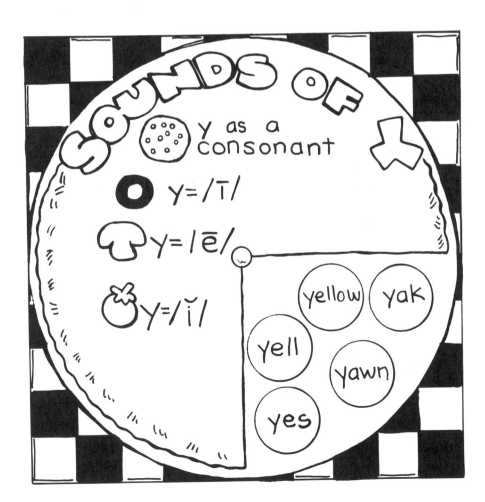

Write Clues words from a Language Mystery on the backs of pieces of an old jigsaw puzzle. Write one word on each puzzle piece, and place the pieces in a large resealable plastic bag. Write Watch Out! words on the backs of random pieces from other puzzles, and place these pieces in the same bag. Invite students to sort the pieces into those with words that fit a pattern and those that do not. Then, have them assemble the puzzle, word sides up, at a learning center. Not only will they get practice with examples of the language pattern, they will learn what words do not "fit" the pattern, too.

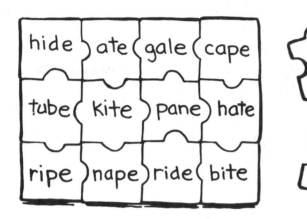

Puzzle-mania

MATERIALS

✓ marker

✓ old simple jigsaw puzzles

✓ large resealable plastic bag

Use tagboard to create a raindrop-shaped tracer for each student group. Discuss as a class the Solution to a Language Mystery, and list Clues words on the chalkboard. Divide the class into groups, give each group a variety of shades of blue construction paper, and have them use the tracer to cut out several raindrops. Invite students to write a Clues word on both sides of each raindrop. (For patterns whose Solution has multiple conditions, have students use a different shade of blue paper for each condition.) Use fishing line or string to suspend an umbrella (right side up) over a class center or from a light fixture. Punch a hole near the top of each raindrop, and tie fishing line or string to the hole. Tie the other end of the string to the umbrella ribs to create a cascade of raindrops. Label the umbrella by writing the Mystery's Solution on a sentence strip and tying it to the umbrella. For easy storage, collapse the umbrella with the strings and raindrops inside.

Raining Rules

MATERIALS

✓ tagboard

✓ blue construction paper (varying shades)

✓ scissors

✓ fishing line or string

✓ umbrella

✓ hole punch

✓ sentence strip

Draw a large five-pointed star on a piece of tagboard. In the center of the star, write the Solution to a Language Mystery. Write on each of the points a word that illustrates the Solution. Cut off the points of the star to create a six-piece puzzle. Create several more star puzzles in the same manner. Create an answer key for the puzzles by drawing a completed version of each one on drawing paper. Put all of the pieces and the answer key into a manila envelope, and invite students to assemble the puzzles during their free time.

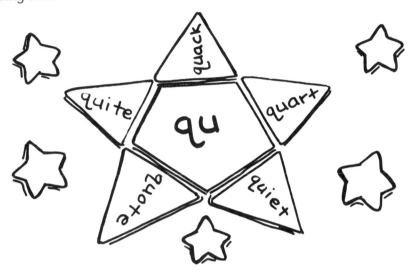

Reach for the Stars

MATERIALS

✓ tagboard

✓ scissors

✓ drawing paper

✓ manila envelope

Each time you cover a Language Mystery, generate a brief class list of Clues and Watch Out! words. Type up each of these lists. Staple the lists and a few pieces of drawing paper inside construction paper to create a booklet for each Language Mystery. Leave a few blank pages between the Clues list and the Watch Out! list. Write the Language Mystery on the front cover. Display the booklets near the front of the classroom. Ask students to add examples of Clues and Watch Out! words to the blank pages as they encounter these words in their reading and writing. Invite students to use these books as reference materials during reading and writing activities, as well.

Reference Books

MATERIALS

✓ stapler

✓ drawing paper

✓ construction paper

Divide the class into groups, and give each group a list of Clues words for a Language Mystery. (Have each group work with a different Mystery.) Have the groups select one member to be the "referee" for the game and give this person the list. The referee begins the game by announcing the language pattern (or the condition of the pattern's Solution) illustrated by the list of Clues words. In turn, group members give examples of words that fit the pattern. The referee's job is to make sure the words suggested fit the pattern and have not already been mentioned. If a student cannot think of a word or suggests a word that has already been mentioned, he or she is eliminated from the game and becomes the referee's helper. The winner of the game is the only person remaining after all other players have become referee's helpers. Invite groups to exchange their lists and play the game again with a new language pattern. Have them select a new referee each time they play.

Single Elimination

MATERIALS

✓ lists of Clues words

After students solve a Language Mystery, generate a class list of Clues words and ask students to copy the list. For homework, have students write an essay or a story that includes as many Clues words as possible. Invite each student to share his or her writing the next morning, and have the class listen for Clues words and count them on their fingers as they listen.

Squeeze Them In

MATERIALS

✓ none

ivide the class into teams, and line up the teams in front of the chalkboard with the first person on each team approximately one step from the board. Give the first person in each line a flyswatter. Write on the board in front of each team the conditions of the Solution for the Language Mystery being reinforced (e.g., *-ar, -er,* and *-or*). Call out a word. The first person to step forward and swat the condition that matches the word earns a point for the team. Have players hand their flyswatter to the next person in line, and continue play. Declare the team with the most points after each student has had a turn the winner.

ivide the class into two teams—an "X" team and an "O" team. Draw a large tic-tac-toe board on the chalkboard. If you are working with a Decoding Mystery, ask the "X" team to name a word that fits the pattern or a condition of the pattern's Solution. For Encoding Mysteries, ask the team to spell a Clues word. For Word-Solving Mysteries, ask the team to define a Clues word. If the team responds correctly, invite a team member to write an X on the game board. If not, the team loses its turn. Repeat the process for the "O" team. The first team to get three Xs or Os in a row wins.

As students prepare to leave the classroom, describe a language pattern for them and have each student name a word that fits the pattern or a condition of the pattern's Solution before being dismissed. Have students who miss a word go to the end of the line and try again, or keep them inside for a brief review lesson. (Note: You may wish to have students spell or define words as well as say them.)

Wash and dry a milk carton for each student. Give each student a milk carton, and assign him or her a Language Mystery. More than one student may work with the same pattern, but be sure the class as a whole works with several different patterns. Have students cut a strip of construction paper to fit around their carton; write their language pattern on the strip; and decorate the strip with art supplies such as paint, tissue paper, dried pasta, and pipe cleaners. Have them glue the decorated strip around the carton. Next, ask students to cut a sheet of writing paper into small slips, write a Clues word for their language pattern on each slip, and insert the slips into the carton's spout. Place the completed word banks at a learning center. Students gain their first reinforcement of the pattern by creating the word bank and gain further reinforcement by referring to the banks during writing activities.

Word Banks

MATERIALS

✓ small, empty milk cartons

✓ scissors

✓ construction paper

✓ markers

✓ glue

✓ art supplies

✓ writing paper

Divide the class into groups, and assign a Language Mystery to each group. Give each group a construction paper vegetable and several construction paper leaves. Have the group members write their Mystery's Solution on the vegetable and write Clues words on the leaves, one word per leaf. Then, have them glue a green yarn stem to the top of the vegetable and glue the leaves to the stem. Staple a strip of brown butcher paper to a bulletin board to simulate soil, leaving pockets wide enough to fit the paper vegetables. Slide the vegetables into the pockets, and staple the leaves and stem to the board above the "soil." Invite students to visit this interactive bulletin board during their free time to read the leaves, guess the Solution, and pull up the vegetable to check their answer.

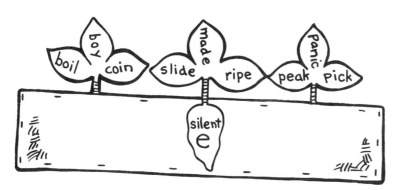

Designate the four corners of the room as home plate, first base, second base, and third base. List Solutions to several Language Mysteries (or one Solution that has several conditions) on the chalkboard. Divide the class into two teams, and invite the teams to choose team names. Select one team to be "up" and line up behind home plate. Have the other team remain seated. As the first student comes to home plate to bat, invite him or her to choose a student from the opposing team. The chosen student "pitches" a language pattern by reading one of the Solutions written on the board. If the student at bat can give an example of the pattern not previously mentioned, he or she advances to first base. If not, he or she is "out," and goes to the end of the line. Each time a team member reaches home plate, record a point for the team. When the team gets three outs, the other team comes to bat. Consider playing this game over an extended period of time or against another class.

Word Roots

MATERIALS

✓ large construction paper root vegetables (e.g., potato, carrot, beet)

✓ construction paper leaves

✓ markers

✓ glue

✓ green yarn

✓ stapler

✓ brown butcher paper

Wordball

MATERIALS

✓ none

Phonics Inventory

Student Name _____ **Date** _____

Directions

Point to each letter or group of letters. Ask the student to tell what sound each letter or letters make. Check those correctly identified.

		Correct?	Comments
Consonants	b		
	c		
	d		
	f		
	g		
	h		
	j		
	k		
	l		
	m		
	n		
	p		
	r		
	s		
	t		
	v		
	w		
	y		
	z		
Short Vowels	a		
	e		
	i		
	o		
	u		
Long Vowels	a		
	e		
	i		
	o		
	u		

		Correct?	Comments
Consonant and Vowel Digraphs	ch		
	ph		
	sh		
	th		
	wh		
	ay		
	ai		
	ee		
	ea		
	ie		
	oa		
Consonant Blends	bl		
	br		
	cl		
	cr		
	dr		
	fl		
	fr		
	gl		
	gr		
	pl		
	pr		
	qu		
	sk		
	sl		
	sm		
	sn		
	sp		
	st		
	tr		
	scr		
	spl		
	spr		
	str		

Upper-Grade Phonics © 2000 Creative Teaching Press

High-Frequency Words Inventory

Student Name _____ Date _____

Directions

Point to each word, and ask the student to read it aloud. Circle each word read correctly.

a	go	more	then
about	good	my	these
all	great	no	they
an	had	not	this
and	has	now	time
are	have	of	to
as	he	off	two
at	her	on	up
be	here	one	use
because	him	only	very
been	his	or	was
but	how	other	way
by	I	out	we
can	if	over	were
come	in	people	what
could	into	put	when
day	is	said	which
do	it	see	who
does	like	she	will
down	look	so	with
each	made	some	word
first	make	than	would
for	many	the	write
from	may	their	you
get	me	them	your

Commonly Confused Words

accept/except	dose/does
advice/advise	emigrant/immigrant
affect/effect	formerly/formally
all ready/already	have/of
all together/altogether	interstate/intrastate
although/thorough/ though/thought/through	it's/its
angel/angle	lay/lie
any way/anyway	loose/lose/loss
are/our	personal/personnel
bow/bough	picture/pitcher
breath/breathe	quiet/quit/quite
choose/chose	shall/shawl/shell
close/clothes	than/then
dairy/diary	their/there/they're
desert/dessert	wear/we're/were/where
device/devise	who/who's/whose

Upper-Grade Phonics © 2000 Creative Teaching Press

Commonly Misspelled Words

a lot
about
absence
acquaintance
address
again
all right
already
although
always
among
angry
animal
another
answer
anyone
apostrophe
argument
asked
attendance
aunt
awhile
balloon
bargain
beautiful
because
been
beginning
believe
bought
Britain
built
business
calendar
can't
caterpillar
caught
cereal
character
chief
children
chocolate

cinnamon
clothes
coming
committee
conscious
cough
could
country
cousin
decorate
definite
desert
dessert
dictionary
didn't
doctor
does
doesn't
don't
early
eight
embarrass
enough
environment
especially
every
everybody
everyone
everything
exaggerate
excited
existence
familiar
family
father
favorite
February
fierce
finally
first
foreign
forty

fourth
friend
getting
goes
going
government
great
guarantee
guard
guess
half
handkerchief
handsome
haven't
height
hello
hoped
hopped
hospital
hour
house
I'm
independence
instead
into
it's
its
judgment
jumped
kindergarten
knew
know
knowledge
laboratory
laid
later
laugh
let's
library
license
lightning
listen

Commonly Misspelled Words (continued)

little	rhythm	too
loose	right	traveling
lose	rough	tried
maintenance	said	trouble
many	Saturday	truly
mathematics	school	Tuesday
money	science	two
morale	scissors	until
myself	secretary	use
necessary	separate	usually
neighbor	several	vacation
neither	sign	vacuum
nickel	similar	valentine
niece	since	very
occasion	sincerely	vinegar
occurrence	skiing	want
o'clock	something	was
of	sometimes	wear
off	straight	Wednesday
often	success	weigh
once	sugar	weird
only	suppose	went
peace	sure	were
people	surprise	we're
picture	surrounded	what
piece	swimming	when
please	synonym	where
potatoes	teacher	which
practice	terrible	white
pretty	that's	who
privilege	their	whole
probably	there	who's
quarter	they	whose
quiet	they're	with
quit	though	women
quite	thought	won't
raise	through	work
really	tied	would
receive	tired	wouldn't
recess	to	write
remember	together	your
rhyme	tomorrow	you're

Upper-Grade Phonics © 2000 Creative Teaching Press

Homophones

accept/except

ad/add

affect/effect

aid/aide

air/heir

aisle/I'll/isle

allowed/aloud

altar/alter

ant/aunt

arc/ark

ascent/assent

ate/eight

away/aweigh

aye/eye/I

bail/bale

ball/bawl

band/banned

bare/bear

base/bass

be/bee

beach/beech

beat/beet

beau/bow

been/bin

billed/build

bite/byte

blew/blue

board/bored

boarder/border

bolder/boulder

bough/bow

brake/break

bread/bred

buy/by/bye

capital/capitol

carat/caret/carrot/karat

ceiling/sealing

cell/sell

cellar/seller

cent/scent/sent

cereal/serial

cheap/cheep

chews/choose

chili/chilly

choral/coral

chute/shoot

cite/sight/site

click/clique

close/clothes

coarse/course

colonel/kernel

complement/compliment

council/counsel

creak/creek

currant/current

cymbal/symbol

die/dye

doe/dough

dual/duel

earn/urn

ewe/yew/you

eye/I

fair/fare

faze/phase

feat/feet

fir/fur

flair/flare

flea/flee

flew/flu/flue

flour/flower

for/fore/four

forth/fourth

gnu/knew/new

grate/great

groan/grown

hair/hare

hall/haul

hangar/hanger

heal/heel/he'll

hear/here

heard/herd

hew/hue

hi/high

hoarse/horse

hole/whole

holey/holy/wholly

hour/our

Upper-Grade Phonics © 2000 Creative Teaching Press

Homophones (continued)

idle/idol	plain/plane	stake/steak
in/inn	pole/poll	stationary/stationery
its/it's	pray/prey	steal/steel
knead/need	principal/principle	straight/strait
knight/night	rain/reign/rein	suite/sweet
knot/not	raise/rays	tacks/tax
know/no	rap/wrap	tail/tale
lead/led	read/red	team/teem
made/maid	read/reed	their/there/they're
mail/male	real/reel	theirs/there's
main/Maine/mane	right/rite/write	threw/through
maize/maze	ring/wring	throne/thrown
meat/meet	road/rode/rowed	tic/tick
medal/meddle/metal	role/roll	tide/tied
might/mite	root/route	to/too/two
none/nun	rung/wrung	toe/tow
oar/or/ore	sail/sale	vain/vane/vein
one/won	scene/seen	waist/waste
pail/pale	scent/sent	wait/weight
pain/pane	sea/see	ware/wear/where
pair/pare/pear	seam/seem	way/weigh/whey
palate/pallet/palette	sew/so/sow	we/wee
passed/past	shear/sheer	weak/week
patience/patients	slay/sleigh	weather/whether
pause/paws	soar/sore	we'll/wheel
peace/piece	sole/soul	which/witch
peak/peek	some/sum	who's/whose
pedal/peddle	son/sun	wood/would
peer/pier	stair/stare	your/you're

Upper-Grade Phonics © 2000 Creative Teaching Press